MAX LUCADO

LIFE LESSONS *from*

ROMANS

God's Big Picture

PREPARED BY THE LIVINGSTONE CORPORATION

THOMAS NELSON
Since 1798

Published in Nashville, Tennessee, by Thomas Nelson. Thomas Nelson is a registered trademark of HarperCollins Christian Publishing, Inc.

Produced with the assistance of the Livingstone Corporation. Project staff include Jake Barton, Joel Bartlett, Andy Culbertson, Mary Horner Collins, and Will Reaves.

Editor: Neil Wilson

First Printing December 2017 / Printed in the United States of America

CONTENTS

CONTENTS

HOW TO STUDY THE BIBLE

The Bible is a peculiar book. Words crafted in another language. Deeds done in a distant era. Events recorded in a far-off land. Counsel offered to a foreign people. It is a peculiar book.

It's surprising that anyone reads it. It's too old. Some of its writings date back 5,000 years. It's too bizarre. The book speaks of incredible floods, fires, earthquakes, and people with supernatural abilities. It's too radical. The Bible calls for undying devotion to a carpenter who called himself God's Son.

Logic says this book shouldn't survive. Too old, too bizarre, too radical.

The Bible has been banned, burned, scoffed, and ridiculed. Scholars have mocked it as foolish. Kings have branded it as illegal. A thousand times over the grave has been dug and the dirge has begun, but somehow the Bible never stays in the grave. Not only has it survived, but it has also thrived. It is the single most popular book in all of history. It has been the bestselling book in the world for years!

There is no way on earth to explain it. Which perhaps is the only explanation. For the Bible's durability is not found on *earth* but in *heaven*. The millions who have tested its claims and claimed its promises know there is but one answer: the Bible is God's book and God's voice.

As you read it, you would be wise to give some thought to two questions: *What is the purpose of the Bible?* and *How do I study the Bible?* Time spent reflecting on these two issues will greatly enhance your Bible study.

What is the purpose of the Bible?

Let the Bible itself answer that question: *"From infancy you have known the Holy Scriptures, which are able to make you wise for salvation through faith in Christ Jesus"* (2 Timothy 3:15).

The purpose of the Bible? Salvation. God's highest passion is to get his children home. His book, the Bible, describes his plan of salvation. The purpose of the Bible is to proclaim God's plan and passion to save his children.

This is the reason why this book has endured through the centuries. It dares to tackle the toughest questions about life: *Where do I go after I die? Is there a God? What do I do with my fears?* The Bible is the treasure map that leads to God's highest treasure—eternal life.

But how do you study the Bible? Countless copies of Scripture sit unread on bookshelves and nightstands simply because people don't know how to read it. What can you do to make the Bible real in your life?

The clearest answer is found in the words of Jesus: *"Ask and it will be given to you; seek and you will find; knock and the door will be opened to you"* (Matthew 7:7).

The first step in understanding the Bible is asking God to help you. You should read it prayerfully. If anyone understands God's Word, it is because of God and not the reader.

"The Advocate, the Holy Spirit, whom the Father will send in my name, will teach you all things and will remind you of everything I have said to you" (John 14:26).

Before reading the Bible, pray and invite God to speak to you. Don't go to Scripture looking for your idea, but go searching for his.

Not only should you read the Bible prayerfully, but you should also read it carefully. *"Seek and you will find"* is the pledge. The Bible is not a newspaper to be skimmed but rather a mine to be quarried. *"If you look for it as for silver and search for it as for hidden treasure, then you will understand the fear of the LORD and find the knowledge of God"* (Proverbs 2:4–5).

Any worthy find requires effort. The Bible is no exception. To understand the Bible, you don't have to be brilliant, but you must be willing to roll up your sleeves and search.

"Do your best to present yourself to God as one approved, a worker who does not need to be ashamed and who correctly handles the word of truth" (2 Timothy 2:15).

Here's a practical point. Study the Bible a bit at a time. Hunger is not satisfied by eating twenty-one meals in one sitting once a week. The body needs a steady diet to remain strong. So does the soul. When God sent food to his people in the wilderness, he didn't provide loaves already made. Instead, he sent them manna in the shape of *"thin flakes like frost on the ground"* (Exodus 16:14).

God gave manna in limited portions.

God sends spiritual food the same way. He opens the heavens with just enough nutrients for today's hunger. He provides *"a rule for this, a rule for that; a little here, a little there"* (Isaiah 28:10).

Don't be discouraged if your reading reaps a small harvest. Some days a lesser portion is all that is needed. What is important is to search every day for that day's message. A steady diet of God's Word over a lifetime builds a healthy soul and mind.

It's much like the little girl who returned from her first day at school feeling a bit dejected. Her mom asked, "Did you learn anything?"

"Apparently not enough," the girl responded. "I have to go back tomorrow, and the next day, and the next . . ."

Such is the case with learning. And such is the case with Bible study. Understanding comes little by little over a lifetime.

There is a third step in understanding the Bible. After the asking and seeking comes the knocking. After you ask and search, *"knock and the door will be opened to you"* (Matthew 7:7).

To knock is to stand at God's door. To make yourself available. To climb the steps, cross the porch, stand at the doorway, and volunteer. Knocking goes beyond the realm of thinking and into the realm of acting.

To knock is to ask, *What can I do? How can I obey? Where can I go?*

It's one thing to know what to do. It's another to do it. But for those who do it—those who choose to obey—a special reward awaits them.

"Whoever looks intently into the perfect law that gives freedom, and continues in it—not forgetting what they have heard, but doing it—they will be blessed in what they do" (James 1:25).

What a promise. Blessings come to those who do what they read in God's Word! It's the same with medicine. If you only read the label but ignore the pills, it won't help. It's the same with food. If you only read the recipe but never cook, you won't be fed. And it's the same with the Bible. If you only read the words but never obey, you'll never know the joy God has promised.

Ask. Search. Knock. Simple, isn't it? So why don't you give it a try? If you do, you'll see why the Bible is the most remarkable book in history.

INTRODUCTION TO
The Book of Romans

At the moment I don't feel too smart. I just got off the wrong plane that took me to the wrong city and left me at the wrong airport. I went east instead of west and ended up in Houston instead of Denver.

It didn't look like the wrong plane, but it was. I walked through the wrong gate, dozed off on the wrong flight, and ended up in the wrong place.

Paul says we've all done the same thing. Not with airplanes and airports, but with our lives and God. He tells the Roman readers, "There is no one righteous, not even one. . . . All have sinned and fall short of the glory of God" (Romans 3:10, 23).

We are all on the wrong plane, he says. All of us. Gentile and Jew. Every person has taken the wrong turn. And we need help.

In this profound epistle, Paul explores all the wrong options and takes us to the only correct one. The wrong solutions are pleasure and pride (Romans 1–2), and the correct solution is Christ Jesus (3:21–26). According to Paul, we are saved by grace (undeserved, unearned favor), through faith (complete trust) in Jesus and his work.

The letter concludes with practical instruction for a growing church, including thoughts on spiritual gifts (12:3–8), genuine love (12:9–21), and good citizenship (13:1–14). The final chapters provide brilliant instruction for dealing with everything from church division to difficult brethren.

Romans is a life-changing letter for people who are willing to admit they are sinners. For those who admit they are on the wrong plane, the letter provides the correct itinerary.

Read it and take note. That flight home is one you don't want to miss.

AUTHOR AND DATE

Paul, who persecuted the early church before his life was radically altered by meeting the risen Jesus on the road to Damascus (see Acts 9:1–31). Paul's letter to the Romans is unique in that he did not found the church, which appears to have been a mixed community of Jewish and Gentile believers who had already become famous for their faith (see Romans 1:8). It is likely Paul wrote the letter c. AD 57 from Corinth, as he entrusted Phoebe of nearby Cenchreae to deliver it (see 16:1–2). Paul employed a scribe named Tertius to compose the letter (see 16:22).

SITUATION

After ministering for two years in Ephesus, Paul sensed it was time to move on to his next mission for Christ. It is likely he had been planning for some time to journey west to Rome and then on to Spain (see Romans 15:22–24), and he evidently wanted to have the Roman church as a base of operation. For this plan to materialize, Paul needed to present to the elders a concise explanation of the gospel he had been sharing with his churches for more than twenty years. The result was a letter that has since become one of the foundational documents in helping believers understand Christian doctrine and the tenets of their faith.

KEY THEMES

- All people are in need of a relationship with God.
- God has prepared for that relationship through his own sacrifice.
- Faith is the requirement of that relationship.
- Forgiveness is available from God for anyone.

KEY VERSES

God demonstrates his own love for us in this: While we were still sinners, Christ died for us (Romans 5:8).

CONTENTS

LESSON ONE

RIGHT WITH GOD

*In the gospel the righteousness of God is revealed—a
righteousness that is by faith from first to last, just
as it is written: "The righteous will live by faith."*
ROMANS 1:17

REFLECTION

The book of Romans offers an expanded and detailed look at God's special plan for the human race. It will show you the "before and after" conditions of your life in relation to Jesus Christ. As you begin this study, consider your lifestyle before you became a Christian. What are some of the major changes that Christ has made in your life?

_____

_____

_____

SITUATION

The apostle Paul wrote this letter to a group of Christians in Rome, the capital of the Roman Empire, to lay out his Christian doctrine after years of missionary work. Although he had not yet visited Rome, he thought highly of the believers there. He wanted to spend time with them, just as he had done with the many fledgling churches around the Mediterranean Sea. This letter was Paul's way of saying, "Here are all the central lessons I would teach you if I were with you." In his opening comments, he describes the glory and power of the gospel of Christ.

OBSERVATION

Read Romans 1:16–32 from the New International
Version or the New King James Version.

NEW INTERNATIONAL VERSION

16 For I am not ashamed of the gospel, because it is the power of God that brings salvation to everyone who believes: first to the Jew, then to the Gentile. 17 For in the gospel the righteousness of God is revealed—a

righteousness that is by faith from first to last, just as it is written: "The righteous will live by faith."

[18] The wrath of God is being revealed from heaven against all the godlessness and wickedness of people, who suppress the truth by their wickedness, [19] since what may be known about God is plain to them, because God has made it plain to them. [20] For since the creation of the world God's invisible qualities—his eternal power and divine nature—have been clearly seen, being understood from what has been made, so that people are without excuse.

[21] For although they knew God, they neither glorified him as God nor gave thanks to him, but their thinking became futile and their foolish hearts were darkened. [22] Although they claimed to be wise, they became fools [23] and exchanged the glory of the immortal God for images made to look like a mortal human being and birds and animals and reptiles.

[24] Therefore God gave them over in the sinful desires of their hearts to sexual impurity for the degrading of their bodies with one another. [25] They exchanged the truth about God for a lie, and worshiped and served created things rather than the Creator—who is forever praised. Amen.

[26] Because of this, God gave them over to shameful lusts. Even their women exchanged natural sexual relations for unnatural ones. [27] In the same way the men also abandoned natural relations with women and were inflamed with lust for one another. Men committed shameful acts with other men, and received in themselves the due penalty for their error.

[28] Furthermore, just as they did not think it worthwhile to retain the knowledge of God, so God gave them over to a depraved mind, so that they do what ought not to be done. [29] They have become filled with every kind of wickedness, evil, greed and depravity. They are full of envy, murder, strife, deceit and malice. They are gossips, [30] slanderers, God-haters, insolent, arrogant and boastful; they invent ways of doing evil; they disobey their parents; [31] they have no understanding, no fidelity, no love, no mercy. [32] Although they know God's righteous decree that those who do such things deserve death, they not only continue to do these very things but also approve of those who practice them.

New King James Version

[16] For I am not ashamed of the gospel of Christ, for it is the power of God to salvation for everyone who believes, for the Jew first and also for the Greek. [17] For in it the righteousness of God is revealed from faith to faith; as it is written, "The just shall live by faith."

[18] For the wrath of God is revealed from heaven against all ungodliness and unrighteousness of men, who suppress the truth in unrighteousness, [19] because what may be known of God is manifest in them, for God has shown it to them. [20] For since the creation of the world His invisible attributes are clearly seen, being understood by the things that are made, even His eternal power and Godhead, so that they are without excuse, [21] because, although they knew God, they did not glorify Him as God, nor were thankful, but became futile in their thoughts, and their foolish hearts were darkened. [22] Professing to be wise, they became fools, [23] and changed the glory of the incorruptible God into an image made like corruptible man—and birds and four-footed animals and creeping things.

[24] Therefore God also gave them up to uncleanness, in the lusts of their hearts, to dishonor their bodies among themselves, [25] who exchanged the truth of God for the lie, and worshiped and served the creature rather than the Creator, who is blessed forever. Amen.

[26] For this reason God gave them up to vile passions. For even their women exchanged the natural use for what is against nature. [27] Likewise also the men, leaving the natural use of the woman, burned in their lust for one another, men with men committing what is shameful, and receiving in themselves the penalty of their error which was due.

[28] And even as they did not like to retain God in their knowledge, God gave them over to a debased mind, to do those things which are not fitting; [29] being filled with all unrighteousness, sexual immorality, wickedness, covetousness, maliciousness; full of envy, murder, strife, deceit, evil-mindedness; they are whisperers, [30] backbiters, haters of God, violent, proud, boasters, inventors of evil things, disobedient to parents, [31] undiscerning, untrustworthy, unloving, unforgiving, unmerciful; [32] who, knowing the righteous judgment of God, that those who practice

such things are deserving of death, not only do the same but also approve of those who practice them.

EXPLORATION

1. What does Paul mean when he says he is "not ashamed of the gospel" (Romans 1:16)?

GOSPEL: SALVATION

2. In what ways does God reveal himself to people (see also Psalm 19:1, John 14:10, 26; Acts 14:17; 1 Corinthians 2:13; and 1 John 5:13)?

THROUGH CREATION, LIFE
HIS INVISIBLE HAND

3. How does Paul say that some people have provoked God to anger?

DENIAL, DESPITE KNOWLEDGE

4. How and why is the truth of the gospel hidden from some individuals?

THROUGH CHOICE

5. What happens when God lets people go their own way?

DESCEND INTO DEPTHS OF DEPRAVITY

6. How does Paul say people can find freedom from the bondage of sin?

GOSPEL = SALVATION

INSPIRATION

Behind him, a trail of tracks. Beneath him, a pounding stallion. Before him, miles of trail to cover. Within him, a flint-rock resolve.

Squinty eyed. Firm jawed. Rawboned. Pony Express riders had one assignment—deliver the message safely and quickly. They seized every advantage: the shortest route, the fastest horse, the lightest saddle. Even the lightest lunchbox.

Only the sturdy were hired. Could they handle the horses? The heat? Could they outrun robbers and outlast blizzards? The young and the orphans were preferred. Those selected were given $125 a month (a good salary in 1860), a Colt revolver, a lightweight rifle, a bright red shirt, blue trousers, and eight hours to cover eighty miles, six days a week. Hard work and high pay. But the message was worth it.

The apostle Paul would have loved the Pony Express. For he, like the riders, had been entrusted with a message.

"I have a duty to all people," Paul told the Roman church (Romans 1:14 NCV). He had something for them—a message. He'd been entrusted as a Pony Express courier with a divine message, the gospel. Nothing mattered more to Paul than the gospel. "I am not ashamed of the gospel," he wrote next, "because it is the power of God for the salvation of everyone who believes" (Romans 1:16).

Paul existed to deliver the message. How people remembered him was secondary. (Why else would he have introduced himself as a slave in Romans 1:1?) How people remembered Christ was primary. Paul's message was not about himself. His message was all about Christ. (From *It's Not About Me* by Max Lucado.)

REACTION

7. How does Paul describe your condition before you accepted Christ as your Savior?

8. How would you describe righteousness to a new believer?

TRUST / FAITH IN GOD'S PLAN
GOD = ALL KNOWING, HIS PLAN IS ABSOLUTE TRUTH

9. Based on this passage, what is required to be right with God (see also John 14:6)?

ACCEPT + BELIEVE, HAVE FAITH
LIVE A LIFE DEVOID OF / AVOID SIN

10. In what ways have you seen the righteousness of Christ transform a person's life?

11. In what areas of your life do your sinful desires tend to interfere with living a righteous life?

12. How does this passage encourage you to live by faith?

LIFE LESSONS

Whether we are new in our faith or have trusted in Christ for years, all of us struggle with the tendency to fall back on our righteousness, our "track record" or ability to do and be good, rather than placing our hope in Christ. Really understanding that Jesus wants our complete trust is an ongoing process. Putting faith in Jesus is a starting point, but it isn't the end of it. Each day is a fresh opportunity to acknowledge and experience living by Christ's righteousness.

DEVOTION

Father, forgive us for being witnesses of your majesty and yet living as though you do not exist. Forgive us, Lord, when we put more hope in the things of this earth than in the incredible promises of your heaven. Have mercy on our hardened hearts. Transform us into your likeness.

JOURNALING

If you recently trusted Christ, what lessons in living by faith have you learned? If you've been a believer for a while, what disciplines have you learned about keeping your faith lively?

FOR FURTHER READING

To complete the book of Romans during this twelve-part study, read Romans 1:1–32. For more Bible passages on righteousness, read 1 Samuel 26:23; 1 Kings 10:9; Habakkuk 2:4; Zephaniah 2:3; Malachi 4:2; Romans 8:10; Galatians 3:11; and 2 Timothy 3:16.

KNOWING CHRIST

All who sin apart from the law will also perish apart from the law, and all who sin under the law will be judged by the law. For it is not those who hear the law who are righteous in God's sight, but it is those who obey the law who will be declared righteous

ROMANS 2:12–13 NKJV

REFLECTION

In the last lesson, you saw how in the beginning people deliberately rebelled, and now every generation experiences the results of that rebellion. Repentance is the first step that begins the journey home, and the gospel offers the hope for that journey. What steps have you taken recently to deepen your relationship with Christ?

_____

_____

_____

SITUATION

Paul was aware that his audience had a divided worldview—Jewish and Gentile—and that he needed to get the attention of two kinds of thinking. In this next part of his letter, he addresses the self-confident Jewish mindset that assumed a special place in God's plan, as well as the Gentile mind that was proudly self-reliant. Both ways of thinking needed to undergo a change of perspective by seeing the human condition from God's holy perspective.

OBSERVATION

Read Romans 2:1–16 from the New International Version or the New King James Version.

NEW INTERNATIONAL VERSION

¹ You, therefore, have no excuse, you who pass judgment on someone else, for at whatever point you judge another, you are condemning yourself, because you who pass judgment do the same things. ² Now we know that God's judgment against those who do such things is based on

truth. ³ So when you, a mere human being, pass judgment on them and yet do the same things, do you think you will escape God's judgment? ⁴ Or do you show contempt for the riches of his kindness, forbearance and patience, not realizing that God's kindness is intended to lead you to repentance?

⁵ But because of your stubbornness and your unrepentant heart, you are storing up wrath against yourself for the day of God's wrath, when his righteous judgment will be revealed. ⁶ God "will repay each person according to what they have done." ⁷ To those who by persistence in doing good seek glory, honor and immortality, he will give eternal life. ⁸ But for those who are self-seeking and who reject the truth and follow evil, there will be wrath and anger. ⁹ There will be trouble and distress for every human being who does evil: first for the Jew, then for the Gentile; ¹⁰ but glory, honor and peace for everyone who does good: first for the Jew, then for the Gentile. ¹¹ For God does not show favoritism.

¹² All who sin apart from the law will also perish apart from the law, and all who sin under the law will be judged by the law. ¹³ For it is not those who hear the law who are righteous in God's sight, but it is those who obey the law who will be declared righteous. ¹⁴ (Indeed, when Gentiles, who do not have the law, do by nature things required by the law, they are a law for themselves, even though they do not have the law. ¹⁵ They show that the requirements of the law are written on their hearts, their consciences also bearing witness, and their thoughts sometimes accusing them and at other times even defending them.) ¹⁶ This will take place on the day when God judges people's secrets through Jesus Christ, as my gospel declares.

NEW KING JAMES VERSION

¹ Therefore you are inexcusable, O man, whoever you are who judge, for in whatever you judge another you condemn yourself; for you who judge practice the same things. ² But we know that the judgment of God is according to truth against those who practice such things. ³ And do you think this, O man, you who judge those practicing such things,

and doing the same, that you will escape the judgment of God? [4] Or do you despise the riches of His goodness, forbearance, and longsuffering, not knowing that the goodness of God leads you to repentance? [5] But in accordance with your hardness and your impenitent heart you are treasuring up for yourself wrath in the day of wrath and revelation of the righteous judgment of God, [6] who "will render to each one according to his deeds": [7] eternal life to those who by patient continuance in doing good seek for glory, honor, and immortality; [8] but to those who are self-seeking and do not obey the truth, but obey unrighteousness— indignation and wrath, [9] tribulation and anguish, on every soul of man who does evil, of the Jew first and also of the Greek; [10] but glory, honor, and peace to everyone who works what is good, to the Jew first and also to the Greek. [11] For there is no partiality with God.

[12] For as many as have sinned without law will also perish without law, and as many as have sinned in the law will be judged by the law [13] (for not the hearers of the law are just in the sight of God, but the doers of the law will be justified; [14] for when Gentiles, who do not have the law, by nature do the things in the law, these, although not having the law, are a law to themselves, [15] who show the work of the law written in their hearts, their conscience also bearing witness, and between themselves their thoughts accusing or else excusing them) [16] in the day when God will judge the secrets of men by Jesus Christ, according to my gospel.

EXPLORATION

1. What reason did Paul give for advising the believers to avoid judging others?

2. What does Paul say was God's purpose for extending kindness toward the believers?

_____

_____

3. What guidelines does Paul say that God will use to reward or punish people?

_____

_____

4. If hearing the law does not make people right with God, what does?

_____

5. How can you tell right from wrong? What guides you in this?

_____

_____

6. What does it mean to have the requirements of God's law written on your heart?

_____

_____

_____

INSPIRATION

I've wondered, at times, what kind of man this Judas was. What he looked like, how he acted, who his friends were. . . . But for all the things we don't know about Judas, there is one thing we know for sure: he had no relationship with the Master. He had seen Jesus, but he did not know him. He had heard Jesus, but he did not understand him. He had religion, but no relationship.

As Satan worked his way around the table in the Upper Room, he needed a special kind of man to betray our Lord. He needed a man who had seen Jesus, but did not know him. He needed a man who knew the actions of Jesus, but had missed out on the mission of Jesus. Judas was this man. He knew the empire but had never known the Man.

We learn this timeless lesson from the betrayer. Satan's best tools of destruction are not from outside the church, they are from within the church. A church will never die from the immorality in Hollywood or the corruption in Washington. But it will die from corrosion within—from those who bear the name of Jesus but have never met him, and from those who have religion, but no relationship.

Judas bore the cloak of religion, but he never knew the heart of Christ. Let's make it our goal to know him . . . deeply. (From *Shaped by God* by Max Lucado.)

REACTION

7. What similarities do you see between Judas and the people Paul addressed in this letter?

_____

_____

_____

8. How does Paul explain the difference between being religious and being right with God?

_____

_____

9. How would you define *hypocrisy*? Why do you think it is so harmful to the church?

10. What are some examples of spiritual corrosion that you see in the church today?

11. In what subtle ways does Satan try to corrode your relationship with Christ?

12. How can you guard against Satan's attacks?

LIFE LESSONS

One area of relentless temptation we can expect to encounter involves our tendency to compare ourselves with others. This type of judging has only one purpose: to make ourselves feel better, superior, and spiritually safe. The Bible consistently points out the dangers and sin of such comparisons. In Romans 2:1–16, Paul shows that comparisons simply deny the truth that we all stand before a holy God as fallen creatures in desperate need of his mercy. When we forget to include ourselves in that picture, we can't see others clearly.

DEVOTION

Father, we have all taken wrong paths and made wrong choices. We know your law, yet we choose to ignore it. We strive to impress others with our knowledge of you when our hearts are far from you. Forgive us, Father. Guide us into a truer, deeper relationship with you.

JOURNALING

What can you do to deepen your relationship with Christ? How can you know him better?

FOR FURTHER READING

To complete the book of Romans during this twelve-part study, read Romans 2:1–3:8. For more Bible passages on developing a relationship with Christ, read Matthew 12:50; John 1:12; 15:5; 2 Corinthians 5:17; Galatians 3:26; and Philippians 3:8.

LESSON THREE

A PRICELESS GIFT

*All have sinned and fall short of the glory of God,
and all are justified freely by his grace through
the redemption that came by Christ Jesus*

ROMANS 3:23–24

REFLECTION

It's easy to question God's dealings with you. His ways are not your ways, and you will never fully understand the mysteries of his justice, holiness, and power. What would you do with humanity if you were God? How would you respond to your sinful creatures? Think about how God has worked in your life recently. What about your salvation is still a mystery to you?

_____

_____

_____

SITUATION

Paul has created a stalemate regarding God's laws. Paul says they are good, but they are also incapable of motivating us to live up to God's righteous expectations. Whether the law is present or not, we can't obey it perfectly, so we are still sinners. It is quite a predicament! But Paul is only laying the foundation for the good news that follows in this section of his letter. As you read Paul's letter to the Romans, note that *justification* refers to God's declaration that we are not guilty for our sins, *redemption* means that Jesus paid the penalty for our sins by dying on the cross, and *atonement* refers to Christ's sacrifice on our behalf.

OBSERVATION

Read Romans 3:21–31 from the New International Version or the New King James Version.

New International Version
21 But now apart from the law the righteousness of God has been made known, to which the Law and the Prophets testify. 22 This righ-

teousness is given through faith in Jesus Christ to all who believe. There is no difference between Jew and Gentile, 23 for all have sinned and fall short of the glory of God, 24 and all are justified freely by his grace through the redemption that came by Christ Jesus.25 God presented Christ as a sacrifice of atonement, through the shedding of his blood—to be received by faith. He did this to demonstrate his righteousness, because in his forbearance he had left the sins committed beforehand unpunished— 26 he did it to demonstrate his righteousness at the present time, so as to be just and the one who justifies those who have faith in Jesus.

27 Where, then, is boasting? It is excluded. Because of what law? The law that requires works? No, because of the law that requires faith. 28 For we maintain that a person is justified by faith apart from the works of the law. 29 Or is God the God of Jews only? Is he not the God of Gentiles too? Yes, of Gentiles too, 30 since there is only one God, who will justify the circumcised by faith and the uncircumcised through that same faith. 31 Do we, then, nullify the law by this faith? Not at all! Rather, we uphold the law.

NEW KING JAMES VERSION

21 But now the righteousness of God apart from the law is revealed, being witnessed by the Law and the Prophets, 22 even the righteousness of God, through faith in Jesus Christ, to all and on all who believe. For there is no difference; 23 for all have sinned and fall short of the glory of God, 24 being justified freely by His grace through the redemption that is in Christ Jesus, 25 whom God set forth as a propitiation by His blood, through faith, to demonstrate His righteousness, because in His forbearance God had passed over the sins that were previously committed, 26 to demonstrate at the present time His righteousness, that He might be just and the justifier of the one who has faith in Jesus.

27 Where is boasting then? It is excluded. By what law? Of works? No, but by the law of faith. 28 Therefore we conclude that a man is justified by faith apart from the deeds of the law. 29 Or is He the God of the Jews

only? Is He not also the God of the Gentiles? Yes, of the Gentiles also, [30] since there is one God who will justify the circumcised by faith and the uncircumcised through faith. [31] Do we then make void the law through faith? Certainly not! On the contrary, we establish the law.

EXPLORATION

1. What does Paul say all people share when it comes to God's laws and his standards?

2. How are people made right with God? What is required of them?

3. How did God demonstrate his righteousness in not just "dismissing" people's sins?

4. How does God's plan demonstrate his fairness toward all of humanity?

5. What should prevent believers from bragging?

6. How has God shown that he is both just and merciful to you?

_____

_____

_____

INSPIRATION

Up until this point in Paul's letter, all efforts at salvation have been from earth upward. Humans have inflated their balloons with their own hot air and not been able to leave the atmosphere. Our pleas of ignorance are inexcusable. Our comparisons with others are impermissible. Our religious merits are unacceptable (2:29). The conclusion is unavoidable: self-salvation simply does not work. We have no way to save ourselves.

So, how does God make us right with him? How can he punish the sin and love the sinner? Paul has made it clear, "The wrath of God is being revealed from heaven against all the godlessness and wickedness" (Romans 1:18). Is God going to lower his standard so we can be forgiven? Is God going to look away and pretend we've never sinned? Would we want a God who altered the rules and made exceptions? No. We want a God who "does not change like shifting shadows" (James 1:17) and who "does not show favoritism" (Romans 2:11).

Besides, to ignore our sin is to endorse our sin. If our sin has no price, we should just sin on! If our sin brings no pain, we should sin on! In fact, we should "do evil that good may result" (Romans 3:8). Is this the aim of God? To compromise his holiness and enable our evil?

Of course not. Then what is he to do? How can he be just and love the sinner? How can he be loving and punish the sin? How can he satisfy his standard _and_ forgive my mistakes? Is there any way God could honor the integrity of heaven without turning his back on me?

There is. "God was reconciling the world to himself in Christ.... God made him who had no sin to be sin for us, so that in him we might become the righteousness of God" (2 Corinthians 5:19, 21). The perfect record of Jesus was given to us, and our imperfect record was given to Christ. "For

Christ also suffered once for sins, the righteous for the unrighteous, to bring you to God" (1 Peter 3:18). As a result, God's holiness is honored and his children are forgiven. By his perfect life, Jesus fulfilled the commands of the law. By his death, he satisfied the demands of sin. Jesus suffered not like a sinner, but as a sinner. Why else would he cry, "My God, My God, why have You forsaken Me?" (Matthew 27:46 NKJV).

Ponder the achievement of God. He doesn't condone our sin, nor does he compromise his standard. He doesn't ignore our rebellion, nor does he relax his demands. Rather than dismiss our sin, he assumes our sin and, incredibly, sentences himself. God's holiness is honored. Our sin is punished. And we are redeemed. God is still God. The wages of sin is still death. And we are made perfect. (From *In the Grip of Grace* by Max Lucado).

REACTION

7. When did you first realize salvation is a free gift provided by Christ?

_____

_____

_____

8. Who or what helped you reach that realization?

_____

_____

_____

9. In what different ways do people try to earn salvation?

_____

_____

_____

10. How was Jesus able to fulfill the commands of God's law and atone for our sins?

_____

_____

_____

_____

11. How would your life today be different without Jesus? What has his gift meant to you?

_____

_____

_____

12. How will you respond to God for being both merciful _and_ just?

_____

_____

_____

LIFE LESSONS

What is priceless can't be bought or earned. Eternal life is just such a treasure. We receive it free or not at all. We could never afford it. We could never deserve it. It's God's gift to us, or we don't have it. But it would be a huge mistake to conclude in this case that what is free is cheap. It cost God a great deal, including his Son's life, to provide this gift for us. There's no room for bragging in our response, but only gratitude.

DEVOTION

Father in heaven, we come to you, aware that we do not deserve to be in your presence. We thank you that you have provided a path for us through the blood of your precious Son. Your saving grace is a priceless gift. Keep us amazed and mesmerized by what you have done for us.

JOURNALING

How can you tell others about the free gift of salvation that God has given to you?

_____

_____

_____

_____

_____

_____

_____

_____

_____

_____

_____

_____

FOR FURTHER READING

To complete the book of Romans during this twelve-part study, read Romans 3:9–31. For more Bible passages on the gift of salvation, read John 3:16; Acts 4:12; Ephesians 2:8; 1 Thessalonians 5:9; 1 Timothy 1:15; Titus 2:11; and Hebrews 5:7–9.

THE FAITH OF ABRAHAM

*He did not waver at the promise of God through
unbelief, but was strengthened in faith, giving glory
to God, and being fully convinced that what He
had promised He was also able to perform.*

ROMANS 4:20–21 NKJV

REFLECTION

With the exception of Moses, no character in the Old Testament is mentioned more in the New Testament than Abraham. He was considered by the Jewish people to be the founding father of the nation of Israel, and they held him in high regard for putting his faith in God and trusting that the Lord would deliver on his promises. Think of someone who has been an example of great faith to you. What are the evidences of that person's faith?

_____

_____

_____

SITUATION

In this next portion of Paul's letter, he makes the case for God having an ancient plan for salvation. Paul begins by tracing the Jewish lineage back to its beginning with Abraham—the original patriarch of the Jewish nation who was not himself a Jew. Paul argued that if God granted salvation (righteousness by faith) to Abraham long before he fathered the Jewish nation, would it not make sense to conclude that God has a plan for the rest of the Gentiles? In this way, Paul shows that God's plan has always been based on faith, not lineage.

OBSERVATION

Read Romans 4:13–25 from the New International Version or the New King James Version.

New International Version

¹³ It was not through the law that Abraham and his offspring received the promise that he would be heir of the world, but through the righ-

teousness that comes by faith. [14] For if those who depend on the law are heirs, faith means nothing and the promise is worthless, [15] because the law brings wrath. And where there is no law there is no transgression.

[16] Therefore, the promise comes by faith, so that it may be by grace and may be guaranteed to all Abraham's offspring—not only to those who are of the law but also to those who have the faith of Abraham. He is the father of us all. [17] As it is written: "I have made you a father of many nations." He is our father in the sight of God, in whom he believed—the God who gives life to the dead and calls into being things that were not.

[18] Against all hope, Abraham in hope believed and so became the father of many nations, just as it had been said to him, "So shall your offspring be." [19] Without weakening in his faith, he faced the fact that his body was as good as dead—since he was about a hundred years old—and that Sarah's womb was also dead. [20] Yet he did not waver through unbelief regarding the promise of God, but was strengthened in his faith and gave glory to God, [21] being fully persuaded that God had power to do what he had promised. [22] This is why "it was credited to him as righteousness." [23] The words "it was credited to him" were written not for him alone, [24] but also for us, to whom God will credit righteousness—for us who believe in him who raised Jesus our Lord from the dead. [25] He was delivered over to death for our sins and was raised to life for our justification.

New King James Version

[13] For the promise that he would be the heir of the world was not to Abraham or to his seed through the law, but through the righteousness of faith. [14] For if those who are of the law are heirs, faith is made void and the promise made of no effect, [15] because the law brings about wrath; for where there is no law there is no transgression.

[16] Therefore it is of faith that it might be according to grace, so that the promise might be sure to all the seed, not only to those who are of the law, but also to those who are of the faith of Abraham, who is the father of us all [17] (as it is written, "I have made you a father of many nations") in the presence of Him whom he believed—God, who gives life to the

dead and calls those things which do not exist as though they did; [18] who, contrary to hope, in hope believed, so that he became the father of many nations, according to what was spoken, "So shall your descendants be." [19] And not being weak in faith, he did not consider his own body, already dead (since he was about a hundred years old), and the deadness of Sarah's womb. [20] He did not waver at the promise of God through unbelief, but was strengthened in faith, giving glory to God, [21] and being fully convinced that what He had promised He was also able to perform. [22] And therefore "it was accounted to him for righteousness."

[23] Now it was not written for his sake alone that it was imputed to him, [24] but also for us. It shall be imputed to us who believe in Him who raised up Jesus our Lord from the dead, [25] who was delivered up because of our offenses, and was raised because of our justification.

EXPLORATION

1. Abraham's life may have been filled with love for God, good works, and obedience to religious rules. But none of these things made him acceptable to God. What did?

FAITH IN GOD'S PLAN + PROMISE

2. How did Abraham receive God's promise? How can others receive it?

THROUGH FAITH

3. What obstacles did Abraham overcome to believe God's promise?

4. What does it mean to have a strong faith? Does faith rely on its source or its object? Explain.

FAITH IS INTERNAL, GOD IS ETERNAL
- GOD EXISTS BEFORE MAN, OUTSIDE TIME/SPACE
FAITH = TRUST + BELIEF + OPTIMISM

5. What words were written for both Abraham and us?

"I MADE YOU THE FATHER OF MANY NATIONS, AND SO
SHALL YOUR DESCENDANTS BE"

6. How has God credited you with righteousness? How do you respond to this act?

INSPIRATION

Henry Drummond writes, "You will find, if you think for a moment, that the people who influence you are people who believe in you. In an atmosphere of suspicion men shrivel up; but in that atmosphere, they expand and find encouragement and educative fellowship. It is a wonderful thing that here and there in this hard uncharitable world there should still be left a few rare souls who think no evil. This is the great unworldliness. Love sees the bright side, puts the best construction on every action. What a delightful state of mind to live in! What a stimulus and benediction even to meet with it for a day! To be trusted is to be saved. And if we try to influence or elevate others, we shall soon see that success is in proportion to their belief of our belief in them. For the respect of another is the first restoration of the self-respect a man has lost; our ideal of what he is becomes to him the hope and pattern of what he may become."

This faith moves mountains of inertia in other people. It pulverizes prejudices and impossibilities. This faith is the fruit of God's Gracious Spirit that sweetens a sour world. It replaces suspicion and distrust with friendship and hope and good cheer. It makes our friends, family, and casual acquaintances stand tall.

Faith of this caliber comes from God. If we lack it, we must ask for it. He urges us to come boldly requesting good gifts from Him (see Luke 11:9–13). He does bestow His Gracious Spirit on those who request His presence and are prepared to cooperate wholeheartedly with His commands (see Acts 5:32). He will not withhold any good thing from those who seek His faith in sincerity. He is faithful. (From *A Gardener Looks at the Fruits of the Spirit* by Philip Keller.)

REACTION

7. How does Abraham's example inspire you to have deeper faith in God?

DESPITE EARTHLY LIMITATIONS, GOD PROVIDES

8. What are some ways that your life and faith could influence others?

9. When was a time when someone else's faith made a difference in your life? Explain.

ARAMIS

10. What are some things that can keep your faith from growing?

FAMILY = Ø BELIEF

11. What do you usually do when you experience doubts?

"WHENEVER THERE IS DOUBT, THERE IS NO DOUBT"

12. What can you learn from Abraham about dealing with hindrances to faith?

OPTIMISM, TRUST

LIFE LESSONS

Almost everyone in Abraham's day, as in our own day, had faith of one kind or another. Some of them believed in idols, others believed in luck or fate, and many simply had faith in themselves. Abraham's faith had a divine object. He had faith in God, and he acted on it. The faith people witness in our lives may not automatically communicate the object of our faith. They will see the effects of our faith. If they ask, we must be ready to tell them our faith rests in Jesus Christ. We live by faith because we live in him.

DEVOTION

Father, you accepted Abraham's faith, and you accept ours today. We do not deserve your forgiveness and mercy, yet you give it freely. Thank you for covering our guilt in the blood of your only Son. Continue to strengthen our faith in you, for your glory.

JOURNALING

How are the people around you impacted by your faith in God?

_____

_____

_____

_____

_____

_____

_____

_____

_____

_____

_____

_____

_____

_____

FOR FURTHER READING

To complete the book of Romans during this twelve-part study, read Romans 4:1–5:21. For more Bible passages on faith, read Genesis 15:6; 2 Chronicles 20:20; Isaiah 7:9; Habakkuk 2:4; Matthew 9:29; 21:22; Acts 15:9; and Hebrews 11:6.

VICTORY OVER SIN

Now that you have been set free from sin and have become slaves of God, the benefit you reap leads to holiness, and the result is eternal life. For the wages of sin is death, but the gift of God is eternal life in Christ Jesus our Lord.

ROMANS 6:22–23

REFLECTION

Habits. The best ones seem impossible to develop. The worst ones show up effortlessly in your life. Good habits disappear in a heartbeat. Bad ones linger on and on. Think of a time when you conquered a bad habit. How did you do it? Describe how this made you feel.

_____

_____

_____

_____

SITUATION

Paul knows that people's tendency to abuse the gift of God's grace runs deep. So, as he moves on to this next part of his letter, he leads off with a question: *Does the reality of God's grace make it possible for people to sin at will without concern about consequences?* Paul's answer is clear: *absolutely not.* Unless we deliberately place ourselves in God's hands and become slaves of righteousness, the freedom God offers us will degenerate into slavery of a different kind. We are all slaves of the ones we choose to obey. So why would we choose to serve the world, the flesh, or the devil, when we have the opportunity to serve our Creator?

OBSERVATION

Read Romans 6:15–23 from the New International Version or the New King James Version.

NEW INTERNATIONAL VERSION
[15] What then? Shall we sin because we are not under the law but under grace? By no means! [16] Don't you know that when you offer yourselves

to someone as obedient slaves, you are slaves of the one you obey—whether you are slaves to sin, which leads to death, or to obedience, which leads to righteousness? [17] But thanks be to God that, though you used to be slaves to sin, you have come to obey from your heart the pattern of teaching that has now claimed your allegiance. [18] You have been set free from sin and have become slaves to righteousness.

[19] I am using an example from everyday life because of your human limitations. Just as you used to offer yourselves as slaves to impurity and to ever-increasing wickedness, so now offer yourselves as slaves to righteousness leading to holiness. [20] When you were slaves to sin, you were free from the control of righteousness. [21] What benefit did you reap at that time from the things you are now ashamed of? Those things result in death! [22] But now that you have been set free from sin and have become slaves of God, the benefit you reap leads to holiness, and the result is eternal life. [23] For the wages of sin is death, but the gift of God is eternal life in Christ Jesus our Lord.

NEW KING JAMES VERSION

[15] What then? Shall we sin because we are not under law but under grace? Certainly not! [16] Do you not know that to whom you present yourselves slaves to obey, you are that one's slaves whom you obey, whether of sin leading to death, or of obedience leading to righteousness? [17] But God be thanked that though you were slaves of sin, yet you obeyed from the heart that form of doctrine to which you were delivered. [18] And having been set free from sin, you became slaves of righteousness. [19] I speak in human terms because of the weakness of your flesh. For just as you presented your members as slaves of uncleanness, and of lawlessness leading to more lawlessness, so now present your members as slaves of righteousness for holiness.

[20] For when you were slaves of sin, you were free in regard to righteousness. [21] What fruit did you have then in the things of which you are now ashamed? For the end of those things is death. [22] But now having been set free from sin, and having become slaves of God, you have your

fruit to holiness, and the end, everlasting life. ²³ For the wages of sin is death, but the gift of God is eternal life in Christ Jesus our Lord.

EXPLORATION

1. Paul has previously stated that God sent his Son into the world so that our sins could be forgiven and we could be reconciled to God. So why shouldn't Christians keep on sinning?

2. How does offering yourself to someone or something in obedience make you a slave of that person or thing? Give some examples.

3. What are some of the consequences of being a slave to sin?

4. What are the benefits of being a slave to righteousness?

5. What change did Paul say should be evident in those who have accepted Christ?

6. How have you experienced the consequences of being a slave to sin? How have you reaped the benefits of being a slave to righteousness?

_____

_____

_____

_____

_____

_____

INSPIRATION

Imagine being thrown in jail on suspicion of a charge, left there, virtually forgotten, while the system, ever so slowly caught up with you. You get sick. You're treated harshly. Abused. Assaulted. Would you begin to entertain that feeling of lostness and hopelessness?

Back to the question: "How shall we who died to sin still live in it?" Who would volunteer to be dumped in a jail for another series of months, having been there and suffered the consequences of such a setting? His point: Then why would emancipated slaves who have been freed from sin and shame return to live under that same domination any longer? ... We have been programmed to think, *I know I am going to sin, to fail ... to fall short today. Since this is true I need to be ready to find cleansing.* You have not been programmed to yield yourself unto God as those who have power over sin.

How much better to begin each day thinking victory, not defeat; to awake to grace, not shame; to encounter each temptation with thoughts like, "Jesus, You are my Lord and Savior. I am your child—liberated and depending on Your power. Therefore, Christ, this is Your day, to be lived for Your glory. Work through my eyes, my mouth, and through my thoughts and actions to carry out Your victory. And, Lord, do that all day long." (From *The Grace Awakening* by Charles Swindoll.)

REACTION

7. Why do you think people *choose* to be slaves to sin rather than righteousness?

_____

_____

_____

_____

_____

_____

8. Why do even believers in Christ continue to struggle with sin?

_____

_____

_____

_____

9. What are the long-term effects of choosing to continue in a pattern of sin?

_____

_____

_____

_____

10. What can a believer in Christ do to break free from sin?

_____

_____

_____

_____

11. What are some ways you can begin each day focusing on the victory Jesus has given you rather than the defeat the enemy wants you to have?

12. How do Paul's words in Romans 6:15–23 challenge your attitude toward sin in your life?

LIFE LESSONS

Before we trust in Christ's power and presence in our lives, sin and sinful habits exercise power over us. Our efforts to control them are largely ineffective. Whether or not we fight, we're in a losing battle. Sin controls us. But when we accept Christ, the rules change. Sin and sinful habits no longer have power, though they relentlessly seek to maintain influence over us and gain our permission to continue their work. Paul tells us that before we knew Christ, we were slaves to sin. But Christ has purchased us and given us our freedom. We can now by the power of Christ say no to sin and experience the power of overcoming sin and sinful habits.

DEVOTION

Father, we know that you have won the victory over sin and death, and we ask you to be the master of our lives. Protect us from the evil one and the temptations of this world. We invite the purifying power of your Holy Spirit to cleanse our lives. May we stay blameless until the day of your return.

JOURNALING

What bad habits do you need to address? What changes do you need to make to lead a godlier life?

_____

_____

_____

_____

_____

_____

_____

_____

_____

_____

_____

_____

FOR FURTHER READING

To complete the book of Romans during this twelve-part study, read Romans 6:1–23. For more Bible passages on victory over sin, read John 1:29; 8:34–36; and 1 John 1:7; 3:4–9; 5:18.

LESSON SIX

NOT GUILTY

There is therefore now no condemnation to those
who are in Christ Jesus, who do not walk according
to the flesh, but according to the Spirit.
ROMANS 8:1 NKJV

REFLECTION

Some days you will find it easy to live in the truth of the freedom and forgiveness you have in Christ. Other days it won't be so easy. You might surprise yourself by "caving in" to temptations you think you've left behind. But Paul writes that you have been set free from sin and are no longer under condemnation! Do you ever wonder if God will continue to "let you off the hook" after sinning again? How do you deal with guilt and shame in your life?

SITUATION

Paul has thus far brilliantly illuminated the message of our spiritual emancipation. We were slaves to sin, but now we are free in Christ. Yet we still struggle. We are painfully aware of our human shortcomings and our tendency to betray what we know is right. How does God bring together our obvious instability with his unchanging nature and character? In this next section, Paul gives us an overwhelming picture of God's grand commitment to us.

OBSERVATION

Read Romans 8:1–17 from the New International Version or the New King James Version.

NEW INTERNATIONAL VERSION
[1] Therefore, there is now no condemnation for those who are in Christ Jesus, [2] because through Christ Jesus the law of the Spirit who gives life has set you free from the law of sin and death. [3] For what the law was powerless to

do because it was weakened by the flesh, God did by sending his own Son in the likeness of sinful flesh to be a sin offering. And so he condemned sin in the flesh,[4] in order that the righteous requirement of the law might be fully met in us, who do not live according to the flesh but according to the Spirit.

[5] Those who live according to the flesh have their minds set on what the flesh desires; but those who live in accordance with the Spirit have their minds set on what the Spirit desires. [6] The mind governed by the flesh is death, but the mind governed by the Spirit is life and peace. [7] The mind governed by the flesh is hostile to God; it does not submit to God's law, nor can it do so. [8] Those who are in the realm of the flesh cannot please God.

[9] You, however, are not in the realm of the flesh but are in the realm of the Spirit, if indeed the Spirit of God lives in you. And if anyone does not have the Spirit of Christ, they do not belong to Christ. [10] But if Christ is in you, then even though your body is subject to death because of sin, the Spirit gives life because of righteousness. [11] And if the Spirit of him who raised Jesus from the dead is living in you, he who raised Christ from the dead will also give life to your mortal bodies because of his Spirit who lives in you.

[12] Therefore, brothers and sisters, we have an obligation—but it is not to the flesh, to live according to it. [13] For if you live according to the flesh, you will die; but if by the Spirit you put to death the misdeeds of the body, you will live.

[14] For those who are led by the Spirit of God are the children of God. [15] The Spirit you received does not make you slaves, so that you live in fear again; rather, the Spirit you received brought about your adoption to sonship. And by him we cry, "Abba, Father." [16] The Spirit himself testifies with our spirit that we are God's children. [17] Now if we are children, then we are heirs—heirs of God and co-heirs with Christ, if indeed we share in his sufferings in order that we may also share in his glory.

New King James Version

[1] There is therefore now no condemnation to those who are in Christ Jesus, who do not walk according to the flesh, but according to the Spirit. [2] For the law of the Spirit of life in Christ Jesus has made me free from the law of

sin and death. ³ For what the law could not do in that it was weak through the flesh, God did by sending His own Son in the likeness of sinful flesh, on account of sin: He condemned sin in the flesh, ⁴ that the righteous requirement of the law might be fulfilled in us who do not walk according to the flesh but according to the Spirit. ⁵ For those who live according to the flesh set their minds on the things of the flesh, but those who live according to the Spirit, the things of the Spirit. ⁶ For to be carnally minded is death, but to be spiritually minded is life and peace. ⁷ Because the carnal mind is enmity against God; for it is not subject to the law of God, nor indeed can be. ⁸ So then, those who are in the flesh cannot please God.

⁹ But you are not in the flesh but in the Spirit, if indeed the Spirit of God dwells in you. Now if anyone does not have the Spirit of Christ, he is not His. ¹⁰ And if Christ is in you, the body is dead because of sin, but the Spirit is life because of righteousness. ¹¹ But if the Spirit of Him who raised Jesus from the dead dwells in you, He who raised Christ from the dead will also give life to your mortal bodies through His Spirit who dwells in you.

¹² Therefore, brethren, we are debtors—not to the flesh, to live according to the flesh. ¹³ For if you live according to the flesh you will die; but if by the Spirit you put to death the deeds of the body, you will live. ¹⁴ For as many as are led by the Spirit of God, these are sons of God. ¹⁵ For you did not receive the spirit of bondage again to fear, but you received the Spirit of adoption by whom we cry out, "Abba, Father." ¹⁶ The Spirit Himself bears witness with our spirit that we are children of God, ¹⁷ and if children, then heirs—heirs of God and joint heirs with Christ, if indeed we suffer with Him, that we may also be glorified together.

EXPLORATION

1. Why did the law, as a list of rules and behavior standards, not provide salvation?

2. How did God solve this problem once and for all?

_____

_____

_____

3. What are the characteristics of a person who lives according to the flesh? What are the traits of one who lives according to the Spirit of God?

_____

_____

_____

_____

4. What happens when the Spirit of God is living and active within you?

_____

_____

_____

5. How does being led by the Spirit change your identity?

_____

_____

_____

6. What does it mean to be a co-heir with Christ? What privileges does that bring?

_____

_____

_____

INSPIRATION

Peter learned the lesson. But wouldn't you know it? Peter forgot the lesson. Two short years later this man who confessed Christ in the boat cursed Christ at a fire. The night before Jesus' crucifixion, Peter told people that he'd never heard of Jesus.

He couldn't have made a more tragic mistake. He knew it. The burly fisherman buried his bearded face in thick hands and spent Friday night in tears. All the feelings of that Galilean morning came back to him. *It's too late.*

But then Sunday came. Jesus came! Peter saw him. Peter was convinced that Christ had come back from the dead. But apparently, Peter wasn't convinced that Christ came back for *him*. So he went back to the boat—to the same boat, the same beach, the same sea. He came out of retirement. He and his buddies washed the barnacles off the hull, unpacked the nets, and pushed out. They fished all night, and, honest to Pete, they caught nothing.

Poor Peter. Blew it as a disciple. Now he's blowing it as a fisherman. About the time he wonders it it's too late to take up carpentry, the sky turns orange, and they hear a voice from the coastline, "Had any luck?"

They yell back, "No."

"Try the right side of the boat!"

With nothing to lose and no more pride to protect, they give it a go. "So they cast, and then they were not able to haul it in because of the great number of fish" (John 21:6 NASB). It takes a moment for the déjà vu to hit Peter. But when it does, he cannonballs into the water and swims as fast as he can to see the one who loved him enough to *re-create* a miracle. This time the message stuck.

Peter never again fished for fish. He spent the rest of his days telling anyone who would listen, "It's not too late to try again."

Is it too late for you? Before you say yes, before you fold up the nets and head for the house—two questions. *Have you given Christ your boat?* Your heartache? Your dead-end dilemma? Your struggle? Have you really turned it over to him? *And have you gone deep?* Have you bypassed the surface-water solutions you can see in search of the deep-channel provisions God can give? Try the other side of the boat. (From *Next Door Savior* by Max Lucado.)

REACTION

7. Jesus' first call to Peter to follow him was accompanied by a miraculous catch of fish (see Luke 5:1–11). Why do you think Jesus re-created this miracle for Peter at this point?

_____

_____

_____

_____

8. How did Jesus show Peter there was no condemnation for those who belong to him—regardless of his past mistakes and failings?

_____

_____

_____

9. How has your life changed since you began your new life in Christ?

_____

_____

_____

10. How should believers deal with feelings of condemnation and guilt?

_____

_____

_____

11. What evidence of the Holy Spirit's control can people see in your life?

_____

_____

_____

_____

12. In what areas do you need to depend more on the Holy Spirit and less on your own desires?

_____

_____

_____

_____

LIFE LESSONS

It is not uncommon even for Christians to want to give up at times. Feeling like a failure is familiar territory for all of us. But Paul's words in Romans 8:1–17 makes it clear that quitting is not an option for us. Nothing will separate us from God's love. The Holy Spirit will help us go on and live in the freedom of forgiveness. He will show us what it means to "try the other side of the boat" in our lives.

DEVOTION

Father, we want to come to you, but sometimes we are too ashamed of who we are and what we have done. We're afraid that we have done something unforgivable and that you will reject us. But Father, your Word teaches that you sacrificed your Son as the atonement for our sin. There is no sin too deep for your hand of forgiveness to reach. Thank you, Father, for the assurance that we are forgiven and acceptable in your sight.

JOURNALING

How do you feel about being judged "not guilty" by God?

FOR FURTHER READING

To complete the book of Romans during this twelve-part study, read Romans 7:1–8:39. For more Bible passages on Christ's sacrifice for sin, read John 1:29; 2 Corinthians 5:21; Hebrews 9:26–28; 10:19–22; 1 Peter 2:24; and 1 John 2:2; 4:10.

GOD'S PERFECT PLAN

If you declare with your mouth, "Jesus is Lord," and believe in your heart that God raised him from the dead, you will be saved.

ROMANS 10:9

REFLECTION

Some people are exposed to the message of salvation through Jesus Christ hundreds of times but never really hear it. The good news is lost for them among many other messages that provide little purpose or hope. Others seem to respond the first time they hear about Christ. Who told you about Jesus and the gospel message? What was your initial response?

SITUATION

Paul was aware that he was walking on holy ground with his writings. The Jewish history he used to illustrate God's amazing plan of grace for the whole world was the same history the Jewish people used as proof of being God's exclusive people. Paul felt great love for his fellow Israelites. He even wished he could take their place under God's judgment if it would ensure their understanding of the gospel. In this next portion of his letter, he begins to highlight God's ongoing plans for Israel, his chosen people.

OBSERVATION

Read Romans 10:1–15 from the New International Version or the New King James Version.

NEW INTERNATIONAL VERSION

¹ Brothers and sisters, my heart's desire and prayer to God for the Israelites is that they may be saved. ² For I can testify about them that they are zealous for God, but their zeal is not based on knowledge. ³ Since they did not know the righteousness of God and sought to establish

their own, they did not submit to God's righteousness. ⁴ Christ is the culmination of the law so that there may be righteousness for everyone who believes.

⁵ Moses writes this about the righteousness that is by the law: "The person who does these things will live by them." ⁶ But the righteousness that is by faith says: "Do not say in your heart, 'Who will ascend into heaven?'" (that is, to bring Christ down) ⁷ "or 'Who will descend into the deep?'" (that is, to bring Christ up from the dead). ⁸ But what does it say? "The word is near you; it is in your mouth and in your heart," that is, the message concerning faith that we proclaim: ⁹ If you declare with your mouth, "Jesus is Lord," and believe in your heart that God raised him from the dead, you will be saved. ¹⁰ For it is with your heart that you believe and are justified, and it is with your mouth that you profess your faith and are saved. ¹¹ As Scripture says, "Anyone who believes in him will never be put to shame." ¹² For there is no difference between Jew and Gentile—the same Lord is Lord of all and richly blesses all who call on him, ¹³ for, "Everyone who calls on the name of the Lord will be saved."

¹⁴ How, then, can they call on the one they have not believed in? And how can they believe in the one of whom they have not heard? And how can they hear without someone preaching to them? ¹⁵ And how can anyone preach unless they are sent? As it is written: "How beautiful are the feet of those who bring good news!"

NEW KING JAMES VERSION

¹ Brethren, my heart's desire and prayer to God for Israel is that they may be saved. ² For I bear them witness that they have a zeal for God, but not according to knowledge. ³ For they being ignorant of God's righteousness, and seeking to establish their own righteousness, have not submitted to the righteousness of God. ⁴ For Christ is the end of the law for righteousness to everyone who believes.

⁵ For Moses writes about the righteousness which is of the law, "The man who does those things shall live by them." ⁶ But the righteousness of faith speaks in this way, "Do not say in your heart, 'Who will ascend

into heaven?'" (that is, to bring Christ down from above) ⁷ or, "'Who will descend into the abyss?'" (that is, to bring Christ up from the dead). ⁸ But what does it say? "The word is near you, in your mouth and in your heart" (that is, the word of faith which we preach): ⁹ that if you confess with your mouth the Lord Jesus and believe in your heart that God has raised Him from the dead, you will be saved. ¹⁰ For with the heart one believes unto righteousness, and with the mouth confession is made unto salvation. ¹¹ For the Scripture says, "Whoever believes on Him will not be put to shame." ¹² For there is no distinction between Jew and Greek, for the same Lord over all is rich to all who call upon Him. ¹³ For "whoever calls on the name of the Lord shall be saved."

¹⁴ How then shall they call on Him in whom they have not believed? And how shall they believe in Him of whom they have not heard? And how shall they hear without a preacher? ¹⁵ And how shall they preach unless they are sent? As it is written:

> "How beautiful are the feet of those who preach the
> gospel of peace,
> Who bring glad tidings of good things!"

EXPLORATION

1. What did Paul say was his deepest desire for his fellow Jews? What was getting in the way of them accepting salvation through Christ?

_____

_____

_____

_____

2. What is wrong with trying to be saved your own way?

_____

_____

_____

3. What part do our thoughts and our words have in our response to salvation?

4. What promise is given to those who believe and confess that Jesus Christ is Lord?

5. How does God's righteousness motivate us to godly behavior?

6. It's tempting to assume Paul's words in this passage were written to evangelists and pastors, but every believer is responsible to share the good news of Christ. What does Paul teach about the way in which this good news is spread, understood, and accepted?

INSPIRATION

The Bible teaches that God was a God of love. He wanted to do something for man. He wanted to save man. He wanted to free man from the curse of sin.

How could He do it? God was a just God. He was righteous, and holy. He had warned man from the beginning that if he obeyed the Devil and disobeyed God, he would die physically and spiritually . . .

All through the Old Testament, God gave man the promise of salvation if by faith he would believe in the coming Redeemer. Therefore God began to teach His people that man could only be saved by substitution. Someone else would have to pay the bill for man's redemption . . .

Thanks be to God—that is exactly what happened! Looking down over the battlements of heaven He saw this planet swinging in space—doomed, damned, crushed, and bound for hell. He saw you and me struggling beneath our load of sin and bound in the chains and ropes of sin. He made His decision in the council halls of God. The angelic hosts bowed in humility and awe as heaven's Prince of Princes and Lord of Lords, who could speak worlds into space, got into His jeweled chariot, went through pearly gates, across the steep of the skies, and on a black Judean night, while the stars sang together and the escorting angels chanted praises, stepped out of the chariot, threw off His robes, and became man! (From *Peace with God* by Billy Graham.)

REACTION

7. What aspects of God's character are shown through his plan of salvation?

_____

_____

_____

_____

8. How are you encouraged by God's plan to save the world?

_____

_____

_____

9. Why is it often difficult for people to follow Jesus?

_____

_____

_____

10. What can you learn from Israel's response to God's plan of salvation?

_____

_____

_____

_____

11. How can you guard against trying to earn God's approval and acceptance?

_____

_____

_____

_____

_____

12. Someone in your life (and maybe even several people) went out of his or her way to share the gospel to you. How does your effort to pass on the message demonstrate your appreciation of the efforts that were made on your behalf? Why is it important to tell others about Christ?

_____

_____

_____

_____

LIFE LESSONS

God's perfect plan involves a two-part response from us: internal belief and external behavior. We accept with our hearts and confess with our mouths. Genuine faith always involves both the inside and outside. It is not just a public formality or a private belief—it's both. And once it begins, it continues. The internal response connects us with God, while the external response confirms our belief and gives others the opportunity to experience the same benefits of God's plan that we have received.

DEVOTION

Father, help us to understand that your plan is based on love—not on our performance. Help us to be captivated by your love and overwhelmed by your grace. Help us to come home to you in that beautiful path that you've already carved out for us.

JOURNALING

How can your external life reflect more of the internal realities of your salvation?

_____

_____

_____

_____

_____

_____

_____

_____

_____

FOR FURTHER READING

To complete the book of Romans during this twelve-part study, read Romans 9:1–10:21. For more Bible passages on God's plan of salvation, read John 3:16; 4:22; Acts 4:12; 28:28; 2 Corinthians 7:10; 1 Thessalonians 5:9; and Revelation 7:10.

CALLED BY GOD

Even so then, at this present time there is a remnant according to the election of grace. And if by grace, then it is no longer of works; otherwise grace is no longer grace. But if it is of works, it is no longer grace; otherwise work is no longer work.

ROMANS 11:5–6 NKJV

REFLECTION

Think of a time you were given a special honor or privilege. Perhaps someone unexpectedly acknowledged a service you rendered, or your children took time to express their appreciation, or your boss rewarded you in some way. How did that recognition make you feel? Now think about the honor of being recognized and called by God. How does that make you feel?

SITUATION

In the next portion of his letter, Paul provides references about well-known Old Testament figures to illustrate God's larger plan. Elijah's appeal to God is recorded in 1 Kings 19:10–18. The prophet Isaiah's prediction that God would punish hardhearted people is found in Isaiah 6:9–13. Paul's words in Romans 11:8 are based on Deuteronomy 29:4 and Isaiah 29:10. He continues to encourage his Jewish and Gentile audience to see that God's plan and offer of salvation ultimately includes all of them.

OBSERVATION

Read Romans 11:1–15 from the New International
Version or the New King James Version.

NEW INTERNATIONAL VERSION

¹ I ask then: Did God reject his people? By no means! I am an Israelite myself, a descendant of Abraham, from the tribe of Benjamin. ² God did not reject his people, whom he foreknew. Don't you know what Scrip-

ture says in the passage about Elijah—how he appealed to God against Israel: [3] "Lord, they have killed your prophets and torn down your altars; I am the only one left, and they are trying to kill me"? [4] And what was God's answer to him? "I have reserved for myself seven thousand who have not bowed the knee to Baal." [5] So too, at the present time there is a remnant chosen by grace. [6] And if by grace, then it cannot be based on works; if it were, grace would no longer be grace.

[7] What then? What the people of Israel sought so earnestly they did not obtain. The elect among them did, but the others were hardened, [8] as it is written:

> "God gave them a spirit of stupor,
>> eyes that could not see
>> and ears that could not hear,
> to this very day."

[9] And David says:

> "May their table become a snare and a trap,
>> a stumbling block and a retribution for them.
> [10] May their eyes be darkened so they cannot see,
>> and their backs be bent forever."

[11] Again I ask: Did they stumble so as to fall beyond recovery? Not at all! Rather, because of their transgression, salvation has come to the Gentiles to make Israel envious. [12] But if their transgression means riches for the world, and their loss means riches for the Gentiles, how much greater riches will their full inclusion bring!

[13] I am talking to you Gentiles. Inasmuch as I am the apostle to the Gentiles, I take pride in my ministry [14] in the hope that I may somehow arouse my own people to envy and save some of them. [15] For if their rejection brought reconciliation to the world, what will their acceptance be but life from the dead?

NEW KING JAMES VERSION

[1] I say then, has God cast away His people? Certainly not! For I also am an Israelite, of the seed of Abraham, of the tribe of Benjamin. [2] God has not cast away His people whom He foreknew. Or do you not know what the Scripture says of Elijah, how he pleads with God against Israel, saying, [3] "Lord, they have killed Your prophets and torn down Your altars, and I alone am left, and they seek my life"? [4] But what does the divine response say to him? "I have reserved for Myself seven thousand men who have not bowed the knee to Baal." [5] Even so then, at this present time there is a remnant according to the election of grace. [6] And if by grace, then it is no longer of works; otherwise grace is no longer grace. But if it is of works, it is no longer grace; otherwise work is no longer work.

[7] What then? Israel has not obtained what it seeks; but the elect have obtained it, and the rest were blinded. [8] Just as it is written:

> "God has given them a spirit of stupor,
> Eyes that they should not see
> And ears that they should not hear,
> To this very day."

[9] And David says:

> "Let their table become a snare and a trap,
> A stumbling block and a recompense to them.
> [10] Let their eyes be darkened, so that they do not see,
> And bow down their back always."

[11] I say then, have they stumbled that they should fall? Certainly not! But through their fall, to provoke them to jealousy, salvation has come to the Gentiles. [12] Now if their fall is riches for the world, and their failure riches for the Gentiles, how much more their fullness!

[13] For I speak to you Gentiles; inasmuch as I am an apostle to the Gentiles, I magnify my ministry, [14] if by any means I may provoke to

jealousy those who are my flesh and save some of them. [15] For if their being cast away is the reconciling of the world, what will their acceptance be but life from the dead?

EXPLORATION

1. Why does Paul need to point out that God has not rejected his people? Why do you think some people had assumed this?

_____

_____

_____

_____

2. What was Elijah's complaint to God? What was Elijah saying about God's plans?

_____

_____

_____

_____

3. What does God's answer to Elijah reveal about his intentions for his people?

_____

_____

_____

_____

4. How do people try to earn God's grace? Why don't our efforts put God in our debt?

_____

_____

_____

_____

5. Why are some people open to the good news while others are closed?

6. Why can we be confident God's grace is for all who will receive it?

INSPIRATION

The fact that God has chosen some to be saved does not mean that He has chosen the rest to be lost. The world is already lost and dead in sins. If left to ourselves, all of us would be condemned eternally. The question is, Does God have a right to stoop down, take a handful of already doomed clay, and fashion a vessel of beauty out of it? Of course He does. C.R. Erdman put it in the right perspective when he said, "God's sovereignty is never exercised in condemning men who ought to be saved, but rather it has resulted in the salvation of men who ought to be lost."

The only way people can know if they are among the elect is by trusting Jesus Christ as Lord and Savior (see 1 Thessalonians 1:4–7). God holds people responsible to accept the Savior by an act of the will. In reproving those Jews who did not believe, Jesus placed the blame on their will. He did *not* say, "You cannot come to Me because you are not chosen." Rather, He *did* say, "You *are not willing* to come to Me that you may have life" (John 5:40 NKJV, emphasis added).

The real question of a believer is not, *Does the sovereign God have the right to choose people to be saved?* Rather it is, *Why did He choose me?* This should make a person a worshiper for all eternity. (From *Alone in Majesty* by William MacDonald.)

REACTION

7. What hope does God offer to all people? How do you know if you are among the "elect"?

_____

_____

_____

_____

8. What do you learn from Paul's words in Romans 11:1–15 about God's sovereignty and your responsibility to respond to his grace?

_____

_____

_____

_____

9. For what things does this passage make you feel grateful?

_____

_____

_____

_____

10. How do you think some people are misled about the true way of salvation?

_____

_____

_____

11. What are some things in which people place their hope for salvation?

_____

_____

_____

_____

_____

12. Why is it important for you to never take your salvation for granted?

_____

_____

_____

_____

LIFE LESSONS

As tempting as it may be at times to ask, "Am I called by God?" the real question that needs to be answered is, "Have I answered God's invitation?" The emphasis we put on one or the other of these questions says a lot about how we think of God. Is God someone who wants to keep us in the dark? Or is he someone who has gone to great lengths to bring us into the light? Does he want us to live in doubt or live by faith? If we let God take care of the calling and focus on the way we respond to him from day to day, we will experience a growing awareness of his voice as we hear him speak powerfully to us through his Word.

DEVOTION

O Sovereign God, you are beyond our understanding. Your ways are perfect, and your unlimited mercy astounds us. Thank you for calling us to yourself and claiming us for your own. Teach us to trust you more, to love you deeply, and to turn to you in humility every day.

JOURNALING

In what specific ways have you responded to God's call on your life?

FOR FURTHER READING

To complete the book of Romans during this twelve-part study, read Romans 11:1–36. For more Bible passages on the way God chooses to save, read Deuteronomy 9:4–5; Romans 2:4; 8:28–29; Ephesians 1:4–6, 11; 2:8–9; 1 Timothy 2:3–4; and Titus 3:4–5.

ONE BODY, MANY PARTS

*For just as each of us has one body with many
members, and these members do not all have the same
function, so in Christ we, though many, form one
body, and each member belongs to all the others.*

ROMANS 12:4–5

REFLECTION

Some of God's best gifts are relationships with people who show you the gritty and practical sides of following Jesus Christ. These people really *live!* They are not stereotypical, and yet they remind you of Jesus. They break the mold, yet they illustrate God's image. With hardly a word they provoke you to live better, sacrifice, and pay closer attention. Their transformed lives direct you to be more like Christ. Who are the people like this in your life? What gifts or abilities do you most appreciate in them? How have you let them know your gratitude?

SITUATION

In most of Paul's writings, he spends the first half of his letter laying a foundation of teaching and then switches to a closing section of application. Romans is no exception. Paul began this epistle by laying out what *followers of Christ believe* and now concludes with *what this means* for each of us. Paul is in effect saying, "Now that you've grasped these foundational truths, here is how to live them out."

OBSERVATION

Read Romans 12:1–13 from the New International Version or the New King James Version.

New International Version

¹ Therefore, I urge you, brothers and sisters, in view of God's mercy, to offer your bodies as a living sacrifice, holy and pleasing to God—this is

your true and proper worship. ² Do not conform to the pattern of this world, but be transformed by the renewing of your mind. Then you will be able to test and approve what God's will is—his good, pleasing and perfect will.

³ For by the grace given me I say to every one of you: Do not think of yourself more highly than you ought, but rather think of yourself with sober judgment, in accordance with the faith God has distributed to each of you. ⁴ For just as each of us has one body with many members, and these members do not all have the same function, ⁵ so in Christ we, though many, form one body, and each member belongs to all the others. ⁶ We have different gifts, according to the grace given to each of us. If your gift is prophesying, then prophesy in accordance with your faith; ⁷ if it is serving, then serve; if it is teaching, then teach; ⁸ if it is to encourage, then give encouragement; if it is giving, then give generously; if it is to lead, do it diligently; if it is to show mercy, do it cheerfully.

⁹ Love must be sincere. Hate what is evil; cling to what is good. ¹⁰ Be devoted to one another in love. Honor one another above yourselves. ¹¹ Never be lacking in zeal, but keep your spiritual fervor, serving the Lord. ¹² Be joyful in hope, patient in affliction, faithful in prayer. ¹³ Share with the Lord's people who are in need. Practice hospitality.

New King James Version

¹ I beseech you therefore, brethren, by the mercies of God, that you present your bodies a living sacrifice, holy, acceptable to God, which is your reasonable service. ² And do not be conformed to this world, but be transformed by the renewing of your mind, that you may prove what is that good and acceptable and perfect will of God.

³ For I say, through the grace given to me, to everyone who is among you, not to think of himself more highly than he ought to think, but to think soberly, as God has dealt to each one a measure of faith. ⁴ For as we have many members in one body, but all the members do not have the same function, ⁵ so we, being many, are one body in Christ, and individually members of one another. ⁶ Having then gifts differing according to

73

the grace that is given to us, let us use them: if prophecy, let us prophesy in proportion to our faith; [7] or ministry, let us use it in our ministering; he who teaches, in teaching; [8] he who exhorts, in exhortation; he who gives, with liberality; he who leads, with diligence; he who shows mercy, with cheerfulness.

[9] Let love be without hypocrisy. Abhor what is evil. Cling to what is good. [10] Be kindly affectionate to one another with brotherly love, in honor giving preference to one another; [11] not lagging in diligence, fervent in spirit, serving the Lord; [12] rejoicing in hope, patient in tribulation, continuing steadfastly in prayer; [13] distributing to the needs of the saints, given to hospitality.

EXPLORATION

1. What does it mean to present your body as a living sacrifice for God?

2. Dwight Moody observed, "The problem with a living sacrifice is that it keeps crawling off the altar." What does that say about our tendency to hesitate in surrendering ourselves to God?

3. What do you think Paul means when he says you should be "transformed by the renewing of your mind" (Romans 12:2)?

4. What tends to hinder Christians from thinking and acting like parts of one body?

_____

_____

5. What advice does Paul offer about getting along with one another in the body of Christ?

_____

_____

6. What does it mean to "keep your spiritual fervor" (verse 11)? How can this help you to continue to look for ways to serve the Lord?

_____

_____

INSPIRATION

Two of my teenage years were spent carrying a tuba in my high school marching band. My mom wanted me to learn to read music, and the choir was full while the band was a tuba-tooter short, so I signed up. Not necessarily what you would describe as a call from God, but it wasn't a wasted experience either.

I had a date with a twirler.

I learned to paint white shoe polish on school buses.

I learned that when you don't know your music, you need to put your lips to the horn and pretend you do rather than play and remove all doubt.

And I learned some facts about harmony that I'll pass on to you.

I marched next to the bass drum player. What a great sound. _Boom._ _Boom. Boom._ Deep, cavernous, thundering. At the right measure in the right music, there is nothing better than the sound of a bass drum. *Boom. Boom. Boom.*

And at the end of my flank marched the flute section. Oh, how their music soared. Whispering, lifting, rising into the clouds.

Ahead of me, at the front of my line, was our first chair trumpet. A band member through and through. While some guys shot hoops and others drove hot rods, he played the trumpet. And it showed. Put him on the fifty-yard line and let him blow. He could raise the spirit. He could raise the flag. He could have raised the roof on the stadium if we'd had one.

Flute and trumpets sound very different. (See? I told you I learned a lot in band.) The flute whispers. The trumpet shouts. The flute comforts. The trumpet bugles. There's nothing like a trumpet—in limited dosages. A person can only be blasted at for so long. After a while you need to hear something softer. Something sweeter. You need to hear a little flute. But even the sound of the flute can go flat if there is no rhythm or cadence. That's why you also need the drum.

But who wants the drum all by itself? Ever seen a band made up of bass drums? Would you attend a concert of a hundred drums? Probably not. But what band would want to be without a bass drum or flute or trumpet?

The soft flute needs the brash trumpet, which needs the steady drum, which needs the soft flute, which needs the brash trumpet. Get the idea? The operative word is *need*. They need each other. By themselves they make music. But together, they make magic.

Now, what I saw decades ago in the band, I see today in the church. We need each other. Not all of us play the same instrument. Some believers are lofty, and others are solid. Some keep the pace while others lead the band. Not all of us make the same sound. Some are soft, and others are loud. And not all of us have the same ability. Some need to be on the fifty-yard line raising the flag. Others need to be in the background playing backup.

But each of us has a place. (From *A Gentle Thunder* by Max Lucado.)

REACTION

7. Why is it difficult to resist comparing our gifts with other believers in Christ? Why is it often hard to resist wishing we had their "role" in the body of Christ?

_____

_____

_____

_____

8. How hard is it for you to be patient when your abilities don't seem to be needed or you are having a hard time fitting in to the local church body? Why?

_____

_____

_____

_____

9. What are some areas of your life where you need to be more patient and seek God's will?

_____

_____

_____

_____

10. What spiritual gifts do you think God has given you? How has this enabled you to be a part of "God's band"?

_____

_____

_____

_____

11. How have you seen your gifts come alongside and enhance the gifts of others?

_____

_____

_____

12. What does it mean to be "transformed" and serve God with all your heart?

_____

_____

_____

LIFE LESSONS

The challenge for a follower of Jesus is never as much what to do as where to start. We lack obedience more than guidance. There are always enough general commands from God to keep us busy for a lifetime. Obeying what we know usually leads to clarity about what we don't know. Most of what God instructs us to put into action doesn't require that we go somewhere else to practice. We can start practicing love, peacemaking, and patience right where we are. These often help us identify our gifts and roles in the body.

DEVOTION

God of peace, teach us what it means to be peacemakers. Help us to cultivate peace between others and you—in our churches, neighborhoods, offices, and schoolrooms. Help us to start today in whatever circumstance we find ourselves. Teach us to rely on you to defend us instead of constantly sticking up for ourselves. Teach us the art of building bridges and not walls.

JOURNALING

How can you offer yourself and your spiritual gifts as a living sacrifice to God?

FOR FURTHER READING

To complete the book of Romans during this twelve-part study, read Romans 12:1–21. For more Bible passages on identifying your spiritual gifts and learning how to use them for the encouragement of other Christians, read 1 Corinthians 12:12–31; 14:1–40; and Ephesians 4:1–16.

TRUE LOVE

Owe no one anything except to love one another,
for he who loves another has fulfilled the law.
ROMANS 13:8 NKJV

REFLECTION

"All you need is love" as the song goes. This may be true, but most people look for it in the wrong places. Since God is the original source and inexhaustible supply of love, those who know God should function as channels for his love in the world. Think of a time when a friend showed love for you in a special way. How did that make you feel? How did you respond?

_____

_____

_____

_____

_____

_____

_____

_____

_____

_____

SITUATION

The last section of Paul's letter to the Romans includes his teaching on the way followers of Jesus should behave in the church and how they are to relate to the society in which they live. These instructions talk about how believers are to respond to hostility from the world and the duties of citizenship in God's kingdom. Paul them reiterates the power of love. In this passage, he describes the nature of authentic love—a love that all who serve Christ should exhibit.

OBSERVATION

*Read Romans 13:8–14 from the New International
Version or the New King James Version.*

NEW INTERNATIONAL VERSION

[8] Let no debt remain outstanding, except the continuing debt to love one another, for whoever loves others has fulfilled the law. [9] The commandments, "You shall not commit adultery," "You shall not murder," "You shall not steal," "You shall not covet," and whatever other command there may be, are summed up in this one command: "Love your neighbor as yourself." [10] Love does no harm to a neighbor. Therefore love is the fulfillment of the law.

[11] And do this, understanding the present time: The hour has already come for you to wake up from your slumber, because our salvation is nearer now than when we first believed. [12] The night is nearly over; the day is almost here. So let us put aside the deeds of darkness and put on the armor of light. [13] Let us behave decently, as in the daytime, not in carousing and drunkenness, not in sexual immorality and debauchery, not in dissension and jealousy. [14] Rather, clothe yourselves with the Lord Jesus Christ, and do not think about how to gratify the desires of the flesh.

NEW KING JAMES VERSION

[8] Owe no one anything except to love one another, for he who loves another has fulfilled the law. [9] For the commandments, "You shall not commit adultery," "You shall not murder," "You shall not steal," "You shall not bear false witness," "You shall not covet," and if there is any other commandment, are all summed up in this saying, namely, "You shall love your neighbor as yourself." [10] Love does no harm to a neighbor; therefore love is the fulfillment of the law.

[11] And do this, knowing the time, that now it is high time to awake out of sleep; for now our salvation is nearer than when we first believed.

¹² The night is far spent, the day is at hand. Therefore let us cast off the works of darkness, and let us put on the armor of light. ¹³ Let us walk properly, as in the day, not in revelry and drunkenness, not in lewdness and lust, not in strife and envy. ¹⁴ But put on the Lord Jesus Christ, and make no provision for the flesh, to fulfill its lusts.

EXPLORATION

1. What is the one debt you are to owe to others? In what sense is this a "debt"?

2. What one rule does Paul say sums up the whole law?

3. In your own words, how would you describe how Paul characterizes true love?

4. What does Paul mean when he describes believers as people who belong to the day?

5. How would you describe the "armor of light" that Paul instructs believers to equip (see also 1 Thessalonians 5:8 and Ephesians 6:13–17)?

_____

_____

6. How can we "put on" or "clothe" ourselves with the Lord Jesus (see also Galatians 3:26–27; Ephesians 4:22–24; and Colossians 3:9–17)?

_____

_____

INSPIRATION

You know your love is real when you weep with those who weep and rejoice with those who rejoice. You know your love is real when you feel for others what Catherine Lawes felt for the inmates of Sing Sing prison. When her husband, Lewis, became the warden in 1921, she was a young mother of three daughters.

Everybody warned her to never step foot inside the walls. But she didn't listen to them. When the first prison basketball game was held, in she went, three girls in tow, and took a seat in the bleachers with the inmates.

She once said, "My husband and I are going to take care of these men, and I believe they will take care of me! I don't have to worry!"

When she heard that one convicted murderer was blind, she taught him Braille so he could read. Upon learning of inmates who were hearing impaired, she studied sign language so they could communicate. For sixteen years Catherine Lewis softened the hard hearts of the men of Sing Sing. In 1937 the world saw the difference real love makes.

The prisoners knew something was wrong when Lewis Lawes didn't report to work. Quickly the word spread that Catherine had been killed in a car accident. The following day her body was placed in her home, three quarters of a mile from the prison. As the acting warden took his early morning walk, he noticed a large gathering at the main gate. Every prisoner pressed against the fence. Eyes awash with tears. Faces solemn. No one spoke or moved. They'd come to stand as close as they could to the woman who'd given them love.

The warden made a remarkable decision. "All right, men, you can go. Just be sure to check in tonight." These were America's hardest criminals. Murderers. Robbers. These men the nation had locked away for life. But the warden unlocked the gate for them, and they walked without an escort or guard to the home of Catherine Lawes to pay their last respects. And to a man, each one returned.

Real love changes people. (From *A Love Worth Giving* by Max Lucado.)

REACTION

7. What are some of the misconceptions people have about love?

8. How is God's view of love different from the world's view (see also John 3:16; 1 Corinthians 13:1–13; and 1 John 3:1; 4:7–21)?

9. Why is it important that you love others?

10. How do you respond to the "unlovable people" in your world?

_____

_____

_____

11. In what ways do you demonstrate your love for your friends?

_____

_____

_____

_____

12. Think of a person in your life who needs to feel God's love. How can you demonstrate God's love to that person?

_____

_____

_____

_____

LIFE LESSONS

When Jesus was asked to summarize the purpose of life, he immediately focused on loving God and loving our neighbors. He stated what Paul echoed in this passage: that genuine love automatically covers the rest of God's commands. This is not a self-centered, little-more-than-emotions love. The goal is God's kind of unconditional love. Once we've learned to love God's way, the other challenges of life will fall into place.

DEVOTION

God, help us to show your love to those around us. Open our eyes to people who are in desperate need of a loving touch. Let our lives be testimonies of your love for us, so that when people see us, they will feel your love for them.

JOURNALING

What motivates you to love others? What tends to prevent you from loving others?

_____

_____

_____

_____

_____

_____

_____

_____

_____

_____

_____

_____

_____

_____

_____

_____

FOR FURTHER READING

To complete the book of Romans during this twelve-part study, read Romans 13:1–14. For more Bible passages on loving others, read John 15:9–13; 1 Corinthians 13; Galatians 5:13–14; Ephesians 5:1–2; Colossians 3:12–14; 1 Peter 1:22; and 1 John 3:11–23; 4:7–8.

LESSON ELEVEN

SUPPORTING ONE ANOTHER

Therefore let us stop passing judgment on one another. Instead, make up your mind not to put any stumbling block or obstacle in the way of a brother or sister.
ROMANS 14:13

REFLECTION

It could be said the degree of peace in any situation is directly proportionate to the degree each participant is willing to compromise. Peace always involves sacrifice. It requires people to consider the interests of others as well as their own. Think of a time when you sensed a spirit of unity among Christians. In what sense was that true peace? How was it maintained?

_____

_____

_____

SITUATION

Throughout Paul's epistle to the Romans, he has delivered a fountain of pithy and practical guidelines for spiritual living. His counsel has alternated between choices and actions by individuals on the one hand and the wellbeing of the body of Christ on the other. He celebrates freedom in Christ but also cautions against a tendency to make freedom the end in itself rather than a means to an end. In this passage, Paul reiterates that God's freedom is not a license to do anything we want but a charge to always consider what is best for others.

OBSERVATION

Read Romans 14:13–23 from the New International Version or the New King James Version.

NEW INTERNATIONAL VERSION

[13] Therefore let us stop passing judgment on one another. Instead, make up your mind not to put any stumbling block or obstacle in the way of a

brother or sister.[14] I am convinced, being fully persuaded in the Lord Jesus, that nothing is unclean in itself. But if anyone regards something as unclean, then for that person it is unclean. [15] If your brother or sister is distressed because of what you eat, you are no longer acting in love. Do not by your eating destroy someone for whom Christ died. [16] Therefore do not let what you know is good be spoken of as evil. [17] For the kingdom of God is not a matter of eating and drinking, but of righteousness, peace and joy in the Holy Spirit, [18] because anyone who serves Christ in this way is pleasing to God and receives human approval.

[19] Let us therefore make every effort to do what leads to peace and to mutual edification. [20] Do not destroy the work of God for the sake of food. All food is clean, but it is wrong for a person to eat anything that causes someone else to stumble. [21] It is better not to eat meat or drink wine or to do anything else that will cause your brother or sister to fall.

[22] So whatever you believe about these things keep between yourself and God. Blessed is the one who does not condemn himself by what he approves. [23] But whoever has doubts is condemned if they eat, because their eating is not from faith; and everything that does not come from faith is sin.

NEW KING JAMES VERSION

[13] Therefore let us not judge one another anymore, but rather resolve this, not to put a stumbling block or a cause to fall in our brother's way.

[14] I know and am convinced by the Lord Jesus that there is nothing unclean of itself; but to him who considers anything to be unclean, to him it is unclean. [15] Yet if your brother is grieved because of your food, you are no longer walking in love. Do not destroy with your food the one for whom Christ died. [16] Therefore do not let your good be spoken of as evil; [17] for the kingdom of God is not eating and drinking, but righteousness and peace and joy in the Holy Spirit. [18] For he who serves Christ in these things is acceptable to God and approved by men.

[19] Therefore let us pursue the things which make for peace and the things by which one may edify another. [20] Do not destroy the work of

God for the sake of food. All things indeed are pure, but it is evil for the man who eats with offense. [21] It is good neither to eat meat nor drink wine nor do anything by which your brother stumbles or is offended or is made weak. [22] Do you have faith? Have it to yourself before God. Happy is he who does not condemn himself in what he approves. [23] But he who doubts is condemned if he eats, because he does not eat from faith; for whatever is not from faith is sin.

EXPLORATION

1. Based on Paul's words in this passage, what were some of the issues causing division among the believers in Rome?

2. How did Paul counsel the Roman believers to deal with these issues?

3. The debate that Paul mentions in the passage over eating food offered to idols may not seem relevant today. But what timeless truths can be found in his words as it relates to doing *anything* that could cause another person to stumble?

4. When should Christians defer to a fellow believer's beliefs?

5. How do you see Paul balance the idea that believers are free in Christ but still have responsibilities when it comes to showing love to other believers through their actions?

_____

_____

_____

6. Why is it more important to maintain unity than to maintain your personal rights?

_____

_____

INSPIRATION

Accepting others is basic to letting them be. The problem [in Paul's day] was not a meat problem; it was a love problem, an acceptance problem. It still is. How often we restrict our love by making it conditional: "If you will (or won't), then I will accept you."

Paul starts there: "Accept one another!" . . . Those who didn't eat [meat] (called here "weak in the faith" in Romans 14:1 NKJV) were exhorted to accept and not judge those who ate. And those who ate were exhorted to accept and not regard with contempt those who did not eat. The secret lies in accepting one another. All of this is fairly easy to read so long as I stay on the issue of eating meat. That one is safe because it isn't a current taboo. It's easy to accept those folks today because they don't exist!

How about those in our life who may disagree with us on issues that are taboos in evangelical Christian circles today? Going to movies . . . playing cards . . . not having a "quiet time" every morning . . . going to a restaurant that sells liquor . . . listening to certain music . . . dancing . . . drinking coffee . . . In various areas of our country or the world, some or all of these things may be taboo . . . Remember, our goal is acceptance, the basis of a grace state of mind. (From _The Grace Awakening_ by Charles Swindoll.)

REACTION

7. What are some issues that cause debates among Christians you know?

_____

_____

_____

_____

_____

8. How can believers handle controversial issues in a way that builds up the church rather than harm it?

_____

_____

_____

9. How can believers show love and acceptance to one another in spite of differing opinions on certain issues?

_____

_____

_____

_____

10. In your opinion, what are some issues that are not worth fighting over?

_____

_____

_____

_____

11. What beliefs are you not willing to compromise?

_____

_____

_____

_____

_____

12. How can you avoid causing fellow believers in Christ to stumble in their faith?

_____

_____

_____

_____

_____

LIFE LESSONS

Paul forces us to ask which is more important: getting our way or living God's way. The cultural surface issues shift constantly, but the underlying ones remain the same. Will we let God help us love one another despite our tendencies not to do so? Will we make freedom mean simply pursuing our desires or a means to pursue God's desires? Ultimately, we must recognize Christ's Lordship over even our freedom.

DEVOTION

We ask you, Father, to protect your church. Keep us from making our personal rights more important than the unity of your church. Keep us focused on the important things that will build your kingdom. Give us the strength to love and accept one another. Bind us together through your Holy Spirit.

JOURNALING

How can you be more sensitive to the beliefs of your Christian friends?

_____

_____

_____

_____

_____

_____

_____

_____

_____

_____

_____

_____

_____

_____

_____

_____

_____

_____

_____

FOR FURTHER READING

To complete the book of Romans during this twelve-part study, read Romans 14:1–15:13. For more Bible passages on accepting others, read Matthew 7:1–5; Luke 6:37; 1 Corinthians 4:5; Galatians 2:6; and James 4:12.

LESSON TWELVE

LET IT SHINE

I have made it my aim to preach the gospel, not where Christ was named, lest I should build on another man's foundation, but as it is written: "To whom He was not announced, they shall see; and those who have not heard shall understand."

ROMANS 15:20–21 NKJV

REFLECTION

Christians have a less-than-stellar reputation for handling conflicts and confrontations. We find it hard to speak the truth in love and to love truthfully. But most of us have benefited from watching someone who knew how to balance truth with genuine love. How has the positive example of another believer who has handled conflict well encouraged you?

SITUATION

Paul's final words in Romans represents a beautiful example of him practicing what he preached. As he concludes his letter, he emphasizes the high regard he has for the believers in Rome and elsewhere who will read and apply his teachings. He expresses his confidence they can handle the hard-edged and serious parts of his letter. He also reminds them of the main themes of God's glorious plan for the gospel and that God has their best interests at heart.

OBSERVATION

Read Romans 15:14–21 from the New International Version or the New King James Version.

NEW INTERNATIONAL VERSION

14 I myself am convinced, my brothers and sisters, that you yourselves are full of goodness, filled with knowledge and competent to instruct one another. 15 Yet I have written you quite boldly on some points to remind you of them again, because of the grace God gave me 16 to be a

minister of Christ Jesus to the Gentiles. He gave me the priestly duty of proclaiming the gospel of God, so that the Gentiles might become an offering acceptable to God, sanctified by the Holy Spirit.

[17] Therefore I glory in Christ Jesus in my service to God. [18] I will not venture to speak of anything except what Christ has accomplished through me in leading the Gentiles to obey God by what I have said and done— [19] by the power of signs and wonders, through the power of the Spirit of God. So from Jerusalem all the way around to Illyricum, I have fully proclaimed the gospel of Christ. [20] It has always been my ambition to preach the gospel where Christ was not known, so that I would not be building on someone else's foundation. [21] Rather, as it is written:

> "Those who were not told about him will see,
> and those who have not heard will understand."

NEW KING JAMES VERSION

[14] Now I myself am confident concerning you, my brethren, that you also are full of goodness, filled with all knowledge, able also to admonish one another. [15] Nevertheless, brethren, I have written more boldly to you on some points, as reminding you, because of the grace given to me by God, [16] that I might be a minister of Jesus Christ to the Gentiles, ministering the gospel of God, that the offering of the Gentiles might be acceptable, sanctified by the Holy Spirit. [17] Therefore I have reason to glory in Christ Jesus in the things which pertain to God. [18] For I will not dare to speak of any of those things which Christ has not accomplished through me, in word and deed, to make the Gentiles obedient— [19] in mighty signs and wonders, by the power of the Spirit of God, so that from Jerusalem and round about to Illyricum I have fully preached the gospel of Christ. [20] And so I have made it my aim to preach the gospel, not where Christ was named, lest I should build on another man's foundation, [21] but as it is written:

> "To whom He was not announced, they shall see;
> And those who have not heard shall understand."

EXPLORATION

1. What was the basis of Paul's confidence in the Christians in Rome?

2. For what purpose did Paul say he had "written boldly" to the believers?

3. What were some of the things that God had accomplished through Paul's life?

4. What are some things that God has accomplished through your life?

5. Why did Paul prefer not to minister where others had already ministered? What might be the positives and negatives of such an approach?

6. What principles of evangelism from Paul's life are you seeking to apply in your life?

_____

_____

_____

INSPIRATION

An electrical storm caused a blackout in our neighborhood. When the lights went out, I felt my way through the darkness into the storage closet where we keep the candles for nights like this . . . I took my match and lit four of them . . . I was turning to leave with the large candle in my hand when I heard a voice, "Now, hold it right there."

"Who said that?"

"I did." The voice was near my hand. "Who are you? What are you?"

"I'm a candle."

I lifted up the candle to take a closer look. You won't believe what I saw. There was a tiny face in the wax . . . a moving, functioning, fleshlike face full of expression and life.

"Don't take me out of here!"

"What?"

"I said, Don't take me out of this room."

"What do you mean? I have to take you out. You're a candle. Your job is to give light. It's dark out there."

"But you can't take me out. I'm not ready," the candle explained with pleading eyes. "I need more preparation."

I couldn't believe my ears. "More preparation?"

"Yeah, I've decided I need to research this job of light-giving so I won't go out and make a bunch of mistakes. You'd be surprised how distorted the glow of an untrained candle can be."

"All right then," I said. "You're not the only candle on the shelf. I'll blow you out and take the others!"

But just as I got my cheeks full of air, I heard other voices. "We aren't going either!"

I turned around and looked at the three other candles. "You are candles and your job is to light dark places!"

"Well, that may be what you think," said the candle on the far left . . . "You may think we have to go, but I'm busy . . . I'm meditating on the importance of light. It's really enlightening."

"And you other two," I asked, "are you going to stay in here as well?"

A short, fat, purple candle with plump cheeks that reminded me of Santa Claus spoke up. "I'm waiting to get my life together. I'm not stable enough."

The last candle had a female voice, very pleasant to the ear. "I'd like to help," she explained, "but lighting the darkness is not my gift . . . I'm a singer. I sing to other candles to encourage them to burn more brightly." She began a rendition of "This Little Light of Mine." The other three joined in, filling the storage room with singing . . .

I took a step back and considered the absurdity of it all. Four perfectly healthy candles singing to each other about light but refusing to come out of the closet. (From *God Came Near* by Max Lucado.)

REACTION

7. Which of the candles in the above story most closely represents your life? Explain.

_____

_____

_____

8. What has helped you to share the message of Christ with others?

_____

_____

_____

9. What has hindered you in sharing the gospel? How can you overcome those obstacles?

10. How does Paul's example inspire you to get more actively involved in evangelism?

11. Why is it so important to speak boldly to others about what Jesus has done personally for you in your own life? How have you seen sharing your story positively impact others?

12. What are some creative ways you could continue to share the gospel?

LIFE LESSONS

We end this study on Paul's letter to the Romans with a few recurring themes on our minds: *How will we treat our neighbors? How will we love those who share our beliefs and those who do not? How will we speak and live out the gospel within the church and to the world?* This letter invites us to return to it often for encouragement, direction, and challenge. It drives us to appreciate all that God has done for us. It reminds us that the more we learn to love God, the better we are equipped to love our neighbors.

DEVOTION

Father, forgive us for ignoring the lost. Forgive us for selfishly enjoying the gift of your salvation without sharing it with others. Forgive us for the times we have kept our mouths shut, burying the truth of your Word for fear of ridicule or rejection. Fill us with courage. Use us as instruments of your mercy and grace extended to a world bound by sin.

JOURNALING

How are you sharing the light of Christ with others through your words and actions?

_____

_____

_____

_____

_____

_____

_____

_____

_____

FOR FURTHER READING

To complete the book of Romans during this twelve-part study, read Romans 15:14–16:27. For more Bible passages on evangelism, read Matthew 5:13–16; 28:18–20; Acts 1:8; 2 Corinthians 2:14–17; 1 Thessalonians 2:8; and 1 Peter 3:15–16.

LEADER'S GUIDE FOR SMALL GROUPS

Thank you for your willingness to lead a group through *Life Lessons from Romans*. The rewards of being a leader are different from those of participating, and we hope you find your own walk with Jesus deepened by this experience. During the twelve lessons in this study, you will guide your group through selected passages in Romans and explore the key themes of the letter. There are several elements in this leader's guide that will help you as you structure your study and reflection time, so be sure to follow along and take advantage of each one.

BEFORE YOU BEGIN

Before your first meeting, make sure the group members have their own copy of the *Life Lessons from Romans* study guide so they can follow along and have their answers written out ahead of time. Alternately, you can hand out the guides at your first meeting and give the group some time to look over the material and ask any preliminary questions. Be sure to send a sheet around the room during that first meeting and have the members write down their name, phone number, and email address so you can keep in touch with them during the week.

There are several ways to structure the duration of the study. You can choose to cover each lesson individually for a total of twelve weeks of discussion, or you can combine two lessons together per week for a total of six weeks of discussion. You can also choose to have the group members read just the selected passages of Scripture given in each lesson, or they can cover the entire book of Romans by reading the material listed in the "For Further Reading" section at the end of each lesson. The following table illustrates these options:

Twelve-Week Format

Week	Lessons Covered	Simplified Reading	Expanded Reading
1	Right with God	Romans 1:16–32	Romans 1:1–32
2	Knowing Christ	Romans 2:1–16	Romans 2:1–3:8
3	A Priceless Gift	Romans 3:21–31	Romans 3:9–31
4	The Faith of Abraham	Romans 4:13–25	Romans 4:1–5:21
5	Victory Over Sin	Romans 6:15–23	Romans 6:1–23
6	Not Guilty	Romans 8:1–17	Romans 7:1–8:39
7	God's Perfect Plan	Romans 10:1–15	Romans 9:1–10:21
8	Called by God	Romans 11:1–15	Romans 11:1–36
9	One Body, Many Parts	Romans 12:1–13	Romans 12:1–21
10	True Love	Romans 13:8–14	Romans 13:1–14
11	Supporting One Another	Romans 14:13–23	Romans 14:1–15:13
12	Let It Shine	Romans 15:14–21	Romans 15:14–16:27

Six-Week Format

Week	Lessons Covered	Simplified Reading	Expanded Reading
1	Right with God / Knowing Christ	Romans 1:16–32, 2:1–16	Romans 1:1–3:8
2	A Priceless Gift / The Faith of Abraham	Romans 3:21–31, 4:13–25	Romans 3:9–4:25
3	Victory Over Sin / Not Guilty	Romans 6:15–23, 8:1–17	Romans 5:1–8:17
4	God's Perfect Plan / Called by God	Romans 10:1–15, 11:1–15	Romans 8:18–11:15
5	One Body, Many Parts / True Love	Romans 12:1–13, 13:8–14	Romans 11:16–13:14
6	Supporting One Another / Let It Shine	Romans 14:13–23, 15:14–21	Romans 14:1–15:33

Generally, the ideal size you will want for the group is between eight to ten people, which ensures everyone will have enough time to participate in discussions. If you have more people, you might want to break up the main group into smaller subgroups. Encourage those who show up at the first meeting to commit to attending the duration of the study, as this will help the group members get to know each other, create stability for the group, and help you know how to prepare each week.

Each of the lessons begins with a brief reflection that highlights the theme you will be discussing that week. As you begin your group time, have the group members briefly respond to the opening question to get them thinking about the topic at hand. Some people may want to tell a long story in response to one of these questions, but the goal is to keep the answers brief. Ideally, you want everyone in the group to get a chance to answer, so try to keep the responses to just a few minutes. If you have more talkative group members, say up front that everyone needs to limit his or her answer to two minutes.

Give the group members a chance to answer, but tell them to feel free to pass if they wish. With the rest of the study, it's generally not a good idea to have everyone answer every question—a free-flowing discussion is more desirable. But with the opening reflection question, you can go around the circle. Encourage shy people to share, but don't force them.

Before your first meeting, let the group members know how the lessons are broken down. During your group discussion time the members will be drawing on the answers they wrote to the Exploration and Reaction sections, so encourage them to always complete these ahead of time. Also, invite them to bring any questions and insights they uncovered while reading to your next meeting, especially if they had a breakthrough moment or if they didn't understand something they read.

WEEKLY PREPARATION

As the leader, there are a few things you should do to prepare for each meeting:

- *Read through the lesson.* This will help you to become familiar with the content and know how to structure the discussion times.
- *Decide which questions you want to discuss.* Depending on how you structure your group time, you may not be able to cover every question. So select the questions ahead of time that you absolutely want the group to explore.
- *Be familiar with the questions you want to discuss.* When the group meets you'll be watching the clock, so you want to make sure you are familiar with the Bible study questions you have selected. You can then spend time in the passage again when the group meets. In this way, you'll ensure you have the passage more deeply in your mind than your group members.
- *Pray for your group.* Pray for your group members throughout the week and ask God to lead them as they study his Word.
- *Bring extra supplies to your meeting.* The members should bring their own pens for writing notes, but it's a good idea to have extras available for those who forget. You may also want to bring paper and additional Bibles.

Note that in many cases there will not be one "right" answer to the question. Answers will vary, especially when the group members are being asked to share their personal experiences.

STRUCTURING THE DISCUSSION TIME

You will need to determine with your group how long you want to meet each week so you can plan your time accordingly. Generally, most groups like to meet for either sixty minutes or ninety minutes, so you could use one of the following schedules:

Section	60 Minutes	90 Minutes
WELCOME (members arrive and get settled)	5 minutes	10 minutes
REFLECTION (discuss the opening question for the lesson)	10 minutes	15 minutes
DISCUSSION (discuss the Bible study questions in the Exploration and Reaction sections)	35 minutes	50 minutes
PRAYER/CLOSING (pray together as a group and dismiss)	10 minutes	15 minutes

As the group leader, it is up to you to keep track of the time and keep things moving along according to your schedule. You might want to set a timer for each segment so both you and the group members know when your time is up. (Note that there are some good phone apps for timers that play a gentle chime or other pleasant sound instead of a disruptive noise.) Don't feel pressured to cover every question you have selected if the group has a good discussion going. Again, it's not necessary to go around the circle and make everyone share.

Don't be concerned if the group members are silent or slow to share. People are often quiet when they are pulling together their ideas, and this might be a new experience for them. Just ask a question and let it hang in the air until someone shares. You can then say, "Thank you. What about others? What came to you when you reflected on the passage?"

GROUP DYNAMICS

Leading a group through *Life Lessons from Romans* will prove to be highly rewarding both to you and your group members—but that doesn't mean you will not encounter any challenges along the way! Discussions can get off track. Group members may not be sensitive to the needs and ideas of others. Some might worry they will be expected to talk about matters that make them feel awkward. Others may express comments that result in disagreements. To help ease this strain on you and the group, consider the following ground rules:

- When someone raises a question or comment that is off the main topic, suggest you deal with it another time, or, if you feel led to go in that direction, let the group know you will be spending some time discussing it.
- If someone asks a question you don't know how to answer, admit it and move on. At your discretion, feel free to invite group members to comment on questions that call for personal experience.
- If you find one or two people are dominating the discussion time, direct a few questions to others in the group. Outside the main group time, ask the more dominating members to help you draw out the quieter ones. Work to make them a part of the solution instead of the problem.
- When a disagreement occurs, encourage the group members to process the matter in love. Encourage those on opposite sides to restate what they heard the other side say about the matter, and then invite each side to evaluate if that perception is accurate. Lead the group in examining other Scriptures related to the topic and look for common ground.

When any of these issues arise, encourage your group members to follow the words from the Bible: "Love one another" (John 13:34), "If it is possible, as far as it depends on you, live at peace with everyone" (Romans 12:18), and, "Be quick to listen, slow to speak and slow to become angry" (James 1:19).

Thank you again for taking the time to lead your group. May God reward your efforts and dedication and make your time together in this study fruitful for his kingdom.

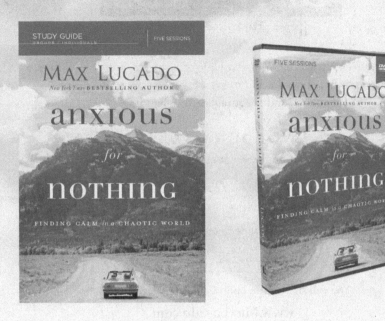